VICTORY
OVERCOMING
OUR ENEMIES

RAUL RIES

SOMEBODY LOVES YOU ®
PUBLISHING
WWW.SOMEBODYLOVESYOU.COM

Victory: Overcoming Our Enemies
By Raul A. Ries

Copyright © 2018 by Somebody Loves You Publishing

Requests for information should be addressed to:
Somebody Loves You Publishing
22324 Golden Springs Drive
Diamond Bar, CA 91765-2449
(800) 634 9165
mail@somebodylovesyou.com
www.somebodylovesyou.com

Library of Congress Cataloging-in-Publication Data
Library of Congress Control Number: 2017952338
Ries, Raul
Victory: Overcoming Our Enemies

ISBN: 978-1-934820-25-4
1. Ries, Raul Andrew 2. Calvary Chapel—United States—Biography 3. Somebody
Loves You—United States—Radio 4. USMC—Vietnam 5. Kung Fu San Soo—United
States—Master 6. Warfare, Spiritual 7. Discipleship, Spiritual

---

This book was edited primarily from Bible studies on spiritual warfare by Raul A. Ries
and published by Somebody Loves You Publishing.

Printed in the United States of America

CONTENTS

A WORD FROM PASTOR RAUL

Christians from all walks of life will face the reality of extreme spiritual warfare. It is important to understand what that warfare entails and to know that Christ has already won the victory when He willingly offered His life on the cross for the salvation of souls. We fight against our flesh, the world, Satan and his demons from the position of Christ's victory on the cross. Our Lord disarmed demonic principalities and powers and made a spectacle of them, triumphing over them on the cross (Colossians 2:15).

We are to be thankful for that victory, *But thanks be to God, who gives us the victory through our Lord Jesus Christ* (1 Corinthians 15:57). It is through His victory that we live the Christian life. It is important to know Jesus did not leave us to fight this ongoing battle alone. He sent the Holy Spirit to empower, teach and help us. In fact, there is no reason why we should not live in victory every day. A Christian should be—*steadfast, immovable, always abounding in the work of the Lord* (I Corinthians 15:58).

As believers, we do not have a choice when entering into spiritual warfare; we come into the battle the minute we accept Jesus Christ as our Lord and Savior. Before we became Christians, we remained oblivious to the enemy of our soul. There was no real battle because we were dead in our sins, embracing our flesh and walking according to the world and Satan—all things contrary to God and His Word, as it states in Ephesians 2:1-3:

> *And you He made alive, who were dead in trespasses and sins, in which you once walked according to the course of this world, according to the prince of the power of the air, the spirit who now works in the sons of disobedience, among whom also we all once conducted ourselves in the lusts of our flesh, fulfilling the desires of the flesh and of the mind, and were by nature children of wrath, just as the others.*

Satan, our common enemy, does not want you to walk with God or serve Him. He is bound for hell (Matthew 25:41), and he will continue to wage his warfare in an attempt to take as many people with him as he can. The Lord has not only delivered you from Satan, but He has provided the spiritual armor and weaponry you need. No matter what strategy Satan chooses to use against you, remember, God has enabled you to fight and win the battle. Learn to use God's weaponry, and you will overcome your enemy (Ephesians 6:10-11).

Unfortunately, I do not see a large majority of Christians living a life of victory. They are not overcoming their enemies; instead, they repeatedly succumb to them. I often find Christians living an empty and frustrated life in the *wilderness*—a place that symbolically speaks of wandering in unbelief and carnality. As a pastor, teacher and evangelist, it is hard to see so many Christians living their lives in constant defeat, unaware of the weapons that Christ has given them to live a life of victory.

Remember, no matter where we are in our relationship with Christ, we must continue to grow in the grace and the knowledge of Christ (2 Peter 3:18). We all need to reach a place of maturity and remain strong in the Christian faith. Think about it, this battle will endure for the rest of our lives. We must never let down our guard but continue to: crucify the flesh, keep ourselves from the world's enticements, and fight to resist the Devil until we breathe our last dying breath.

As a Marine, I have gained a unique outlook regarding spiritual warfare. I gauge the battle through the eyes and experiences of a soldier at war. I believe with all my heart I have obtained a clear vantage point, as I can clearly see the many comparisons. I hope these insightful contrasts, coupled with biblical truths, will equip and encourage you in engaging the enemy in spiritual warfare.

Never let Satan rob you of an amazing life in Christ; walking in victory: *Watch, stand fast in the faith, be brave, be strong* (1 Corinthians 16:13).

Raul Ries

Chapter 1

WHAT IS SPIRITUAL WARFARE?

For we do not wrestle against flesh and blood, but against principalities, against powers, against the rulers of the darkness of this age, against spiritual hosts of wickedness in the heavenly places.
EPHESIANS 6:12

Before I gave my life to the Lord and became a Christian, I was in the United States Marine Corps and fought in the Vietnam War. It was a long, hard and controversial war that officially started on November 1, 1955, and ended April 30, 1975. Before being sent to Vietnam, at the young age of 19, I trained with the Marine Corps in jungle warfare and with every weapon you could possibly use in the war.

I thought I was ready for anything, but when I arrived on the Vietnam battlefield in 1966, nothing was what I expected, and things changed drastically. As soon as my boots hit the ground, I was in a real battle—taking fire from the enemy. Immediately, I had to defend myself. I learned really fast, no matter how much training I had received before war, it was not the same once I was engaged in a real battle.

With first-hand experience on the battlefield, I believed I knew all about warfare; but after accepting Christ as my Savior, I realized I was fighting a very different battle. I understood combat, but a firefight in Vietnam could not have prepared me for the spiritual battle I would face as a Christian. Spiritual warfare is not a physical battle, where a man fighting could be left maimed or even killed. It is a much greater warfare, with an invisible enemy who would like nothing more than to destroy my soul and take me to hell. That is the high price of defeat—your very soul, separated from God, cast out into utter darkness and having damnation for all eternity!

The Dictionary of Biblical Themes, by Martin H. Manser, defines spiritual warfare as, " . . . the struggle against the forces of evil, which is a constant feature of the life of faith. Scripture locates the origins of spiritual warfare in the rebellion of Satan and his angels against God and affirms the hope of God's final victory over such forces through Jesus Christ's death and resurrection."

SATAN'S ANGELIC REVOLT

Spiritual warfare first began in heaven. The Bible tells us that Satan, in pride, rebelled against the Lord. At first, he was a stunningly beautiful, perfect angel, created by God. Scripture tells us he was the *anointed cherub who covers*—a powerful angel who was the chief guardian of the holy throne of God. With his heart lifted up in pride he made this bold declaration:

> *"For you have said in your heart: 'I will ascend into heaven, I will exalt my throne above the stars of God; I will also sit on the mount of the congregation on the farthest sides of the north; I will ascend above the heights of the clouds, I will be like the Most High.'"*
>
> ISAIAH 14:13-14

Ezekiel 28:12-14 describes him:

> *"... You were the seal of perfection, full of wisdom and perfect in beauty. You were in Eden, the garden of God; every precious stone was your covering: the sardius, topaz, and diamond, beryl, onyx, and jasper, sapphire, turquoise, and emerald with gold. The workmanship of your timbrels and pipes was prepared for you on the day you were created. You were the anointed cherub who covers; I established you ..."*

Scholars believe that the precious stones relate to the stones on the garment of the high priests who alone could enter into the holy place in the tabernacle, to do intercession for God's people, in the wilderness. It seems

11

that he may also have been the chief worshiper around the throne of God, as instruments of worship were built into him. Imagine, he forgot he was a created being of God and could not ascend above God, the Creator. Although he was created perfect, he allowed sin to enter in: "*You were perfect in your ways from the day you were created, till iniquity was found in you*" (Ezekiel 28:15).

When Satan fell into sin, he did not fall alone. He deceived one-third of God's heavenly angels and took them with him. He became the ruler of demons:

> *And war broke out in heaven: Michael and his angels fought with the dragon; and the dragon and his angels fought, but they did not prevail, nor was a place found for them in heaven any longer. So the great dragon was cast out, that serpent of old, called the Devil and Satan, who deceives the whole world; he was cast to the earth, and his angels were cast out with him.*
>
> REVELATION 12:7-9

Satan is a master deceiver. Not only did he deceive one-third of the angels from heaven into rebelling against God, he now attempts to deceive mankind, whom God has created and who now inhabits the earth. Satan encountered Eve in the Garden of Eden and used his crafty schemes, as he sought to deceive her.

EVE ENCOUNTERS DECEPTION

Adam and Eve were created in the image of God—perfect and without sin. Satan used a serpent for his deception against the woman, the weaker vessel, who, at the time, was alone without Adam in the Garden of Eden. Notice Satan's subtle attack in Genesis 3:1:

Now the serpent was more cunning than any beast of the field which the Lord God had made. And he said to the woman, "Has God indeed said, 'You shall not eat of every tree of the garden?'"

The word *serpent* is one of the titles of Satan. Other titles for Satan are found in Revelation 12:9, *So the great dragon was cast out, that serpent of old, called the Devil and Satan, who deceives the whole world . . .* Notice, Satan is also referred to as a *dragon*. The Greek word *drákōn* is a very interesting word because it was probably an alternate form of *derkomai* meaning "to look" or the "seeing one," a fabulous kind of serpent with the ability to fascinate. It could accurately and cunningly spot its prey. Various commentators believe, before the fall of mankind, the serpent actually stood upright, perhaps walking on two feet. It was not until the curse that the serpent was put on his belly (Genesis 3:14). Satan used the serpent to come into the Garden of Eden, and deceive the woman.

Satan's primary assault was to draw Eve into a conversation that he might challenge the Word of God. Notice in Genesis 3:1 how he raised a question that caused doubt in the mind of Eve: *And he said to the woman, "Has God indeed said, 'You shall not eat of every tree of the garden?' "*

She was now fully engaged in conversation with the serpent and responded to him *" . . . We may eat the fruit of the trees of the garden; but of the fruit of the tree which is in the midst of the garden, God has said, 'You shall not eat it, nor shall you touch it, lest you die' "* (Genesis 3:2-3).

Eve added to the Word of God. The Lord never said they could not touch it. Satan took full advantage of the situation, because he knew she did not speak God's Word accurately.

Immediately, he attacked her mind with his lies and deception. He twisted the Word of God and placed even more distrust and doubt into her intellect: *Then the serpent said to the woman, "You will not surely die. For God knows that in the day you eat of it your eyes will be opened, and you will be like God, knowing good and evil"* (Genesis 3:4-5).

Everything God had created, along with His commands given to Adam and Eve, were for their benefit. But Satan made Eve believe God was punishing them and keeping something good from them. He told enough truth, mixed with lies, to cause her to disbelieve the Lord.

Eve had the God given freedom to choose to obey or not to obey God's command. She disobeyed the Lord:

So when the woman saw that the tree was good for food, that it was pleasant to the eyes, and a tree desirable to make one wise, she took of its fruit and ate. She also gave to her husband with her, and he ate. Then the eyes of both of them were opened, and they knew that they were naked; and they sewed fig leaves together and made themselves coverings.

GENESIS 3:6-7

When sin entered for the first time into Adam's and Eve's lives, shame was recognized. Sin always brings shame. Before they fell into sin, they did not even know they were naked. There was no sense of embarrassment of their bodies being unclothed. Now, not only did they know they were naked, but they were fully aware they had sinned against God: *And they heard the sound of the Lord God walking in the garden in the cool of the day, and Adam and his wife hid themselves from the presence of the Lord God among the trees of the garden* (Genesis 3:8).

Having enjoyed close fellowship with God, they now hid from Him because of their sin. They thought, *If we hide in the trees of the garden, God cannot see us.* But God is omnipresent; He sees all things—He hears all things. Notice, they had succumbed to Satan's temptation, and now their intimate times with the Lord were severed.

Even though Adam and Eve had been deceived by Satan, God reached out to them in love. In Genesis 3:9 He spoke to Adam: *Then the Lord God called to Adam and said to him, "Where are you?"* This was not an angry God who harshly called out to Adam. The LORD spoke with the soft tone of a father, as if calling out for his lost child.

God's heart was crushed because Adam had broken fellowship with Him. God is holy and just, and even though He loved Adam and Eve, He could not ignore their sinful disobedience. After He explained the penalty for their sin, God exchanged their perishable fig leaf coverings by providing a blood sacrifice for their sin and covered their nakedness. *Also for Adam and his wife the LORD God made tunics of skin, and clothed them* (Genesis 3:21).

God desired to restore fellowship with Adam and Eve, but they had to face the consequences of their sin. Adam's and Eve's sin had separated them from God, and, as a result the Lord had to remove them from the Garden of Eden. Cherubim guarded the entrance so they would not give in to temptation again: *So He drove out the man; and He placed cherubim at the east of the garden of Eden, and a flaming sword which turned every way, to guard the way to the tree of life* (Genesis 3:24).

Now that we have closely examined Satan's strategy against Adam and Eve, perhaps you will begin to recognize some of the same kind of spiritual warfare that has happened in your own life. I hope that you will begin to understand these demonic encounters and learn how to defend yourself against these ongoing attacks.

For instance, has Satan ever tried to bring doubt into your mind? I think of all the Christians who constantly doubt their salvation. Even when they come to church the enemy beats them up. During the entire Bible study, he condemns them as they are convicted over their sin. He is constantly whispering in their ears, trying to convince them they are not saved. So these believers think they have to go forward at the altar call to be saved again. You can only be saved one time, but they will go up to the altar call every week, because they are battling with all these doubts in their minds.

The enemy will also tell lies to make you doubt the promises and character of God. Remember, he will twist the Word of God just enough to change its true meaning; that is why he is called "the father of lies" (John 8:44). He loves to distort God's Word in order to make you fall into sin. Often his attempts are successful. When you are in a time of trial, he will place a thought in your mind that God does not love you. When the Devil begins to tell you lies and you start to believe him, recognize that you are in a spiritual battle.

What about when we sin? Sin will always stir up shame in our hearts, causing us to hide from the Lord. Satan, at the same time, tries to convince us that we failed God—big time.

He makes us believe we can never come back to the Lord or return to church.

Many people have the wrong concept of God and see Him as an angry God looking to consume and destroy them. However, it is quite the opposite; God wants to immediately restore us back into fellowship with Him. The moment we leave, He already misses us! He will always continue pursuing His children. Remember, we are the ones to walk away from the Lord—*He never leaves us or forsakes us*. If only we understood God's character and the way He feels about us when we fail, then perhaps, instead of hiding, we would draw near to Him and readily confess our sins. Always remember conviction should always lead us to Christ to ask His forgiveness. First John 1:9 tells us: *If we confess our sins, He is faithful and just to forgive us our sins and to cleanse us from all unrighteousness.*

There is an important lesson to be learned in Genesis 3:9, when God called out to Adam as he stayed hidden from Him: *Then the Lord God called to Adam and said to him, "Where are you?"* It is very unfortunate that many preachers have taught this passage of Scripture, as if God was very angry with Adam—similar to how your father would reprimand you as a child when you did something wrong. You would hide in fear because your dad was going to use the belt, and you knew you were going to be punished. This was not God's heart attitude towards Adam at all.

In fact, when my son Ryan got into drugs, many times after preaching a service, I would go out into the streets looking for him. I was faithfully preaching the Gospel when my own son was nowhere to be found. As a father, I pursued my son. I was worried and heartbroken. I did not know if I would find him, and if I did, would he be alive or dead? It was one of the most agonizing times of my life.

This is the way God is with each and every one of us. We are His children, and He will pursue us when we stray away from Him. He has the character of a loving father, not an angry father. It is important to understand the truth about God's character and His desire for the backslidden Christian to return into fellowship with Him and for us to be saved. God does not want anyone to go to hell; His will is for us to be saved: *The Lord is not slack concerning His promise, as some count slackness, but is longsuffering toward us, not willing that any should perish but that all should come to repentance* (2 Peter 3:9).

THE CONQUEST OF CHRIST

There is an incredible promise that we cannot overlook in Genesis 3:15. God gave a prophetical promise to Adam and Eve concerning the Messiah. There would be a battle between Christ and Satan: *"And I will put enmity between you* [the serpent] *and the woman, and between your seed and her Seed* [Christ]; *He shall bruise your head, and you shall bruise His heel."*

This prophecy foretold of Christ's human birth, when He came down from heaven and became the Seed in the womb of Mary, who was a virgin. Jesus was sinless and complete deity—God in the flesh. In dying on the cross, Christ would crush Satan under His feet. The power of sin and death would be broken. Christ willingly provided His blood as a sacrifice to take away our sin once and for all! Imagine, before the world even began, the Godhead had a prearranged plan of salvation—*He* [Christ] *indeed was foreordained before the foundation of the world* . . . (1 Peter 1:20). This truth is a foundational crux of the Gospel message—Christ came, died and rose again.

From the very beginning, in the Book of Genesis, we find that Satan waged a spiritual warfare against mankind. We also see that God had a plan before the foundation of the world to counterattack and defeat him. This is vitally important to know as believers. Christ, in His conquest fulfilled the prophecy of Genesis 3:15 and won the victory over Satan when He died on the cross. I want to assure you that Satan, our greatest enemy, was then utterly defeated! Pastor, Bible teacher and author Warren Wiersbe wrote: "Remember you are not fighting for victory, but from victory, for Jesus Christ has already defeated Satan!"

Today, there is still an ongoing battle for the life and the soul of every man and woman. Imagine the magnitude of Adam's and Eve's sin when they lost their spiritual battle. It resulted in all of mankind being born in sin. The entire human race has inherited a sinful nature. Every person born will not only experience physical death, but spiritual death as well. If God had not intervened, this would have meant, throughout all eternity, mankind would remain separated from Him in the Lake of Fire.

Thank God for the Gospel! Remember, God is the Just Judge; everyone gets a chance in this life to accept Christ as their personal Savior. God created us with the freedom of choice; we can either accept or reject the way of salvation that God has provided through His Son, Jesus Christ.

LIGHT OVERCOMES DARKNESS

Before we take a closer look at the spiritual warfare we will experience in life, I want you to know one thing—if you are a *child of the light*, you do not have to worry about demonic darkness. There is too much time spent talking about Satan and his demons. Many people focus on Satan and forget to look up and focus on the Lord. Christians need to constantly fix their sight on Christ's victory won for us on the cross to live the Christian life.

Believers are *in* Christ Jesus because of what He has already done for us on the cross. Satan can mess with Christians, but let us be mindful that we have the power and authority, through

Jesus, to defeat him. I want you to know that you do not have to be afraid of the darkness. First John 4:4 tells us: *You are of God, little children, and have overcome them, because He who is in you is greater than he who is in the world.*

When you are in a dark room, what do you do to get rid of the darkness? Simple, you just turn on the light and the darkness is gone. That is how it is when Christ comes into your life. If you are dealing with the workers of darkness, as the enemy comes against you, call upon the name of Jesus, and the darkness will flee. Darkness has to flee because Jesus is the Light, and He dispels the darkness. Jesus told all the people about Him: *". . . I am the light of the world. He who follows Me shall not walk in darkness, but have the light of life"* (John 8:12).

A common mistake Christians make, after they accept Jesus as their Savior, is they immediately think all their problems and trials will go away—do not believe it or allow anyone to deceive you. Once we come to Christ, the battle for your soul begins, but the rewards are eternal, it is worth the fight.

Remember, when we get saved, we are entering into a fierce battle with a fierce enemy. We have given God our soul, but the enemy, Satan, wants to win back our soul—so just like a soldier in warfare, we need to train and get ready to engage the enemy. If we learn how to be spiritually armed, then we will be completely prepared for his attacks. In 2 Timothy 2:3,

Paul tells us: *You therefore must endure hardship as a good soldier of Jesus Christ.* This is a constant experience for the child of God; we all have to go through hardship as a soldier of Christ. We are called to be prepared for battle.

The Christian life is a conflict. Yes, the battle has to be fought daily; yet, we should not be discouraged. Like Paul said in Romans 8:31: *What then shall we say to these things? If God is for us, who can be against us?* Think about that. The call for every Christian is to have courage, determination and undaunted hope in Jesus Christ. When we remember that God is for us, our problems and conflicts become very small. As we continue to study the Scriptures, we will be encouraged and come to understand that He has a perfect plan for our lives.

Chapter 2

THE WATCHMAN

"So you, son of man: I have made you a watchman
for the house of Israel; therefore you shall hear
a word from My mouth and warn them for Me."
EZEKIEL 33:7

Watch is actually a military term for a period of time during which a Marine performs the prescribed duties, beginning when he is posted and terminating when he is relieved by a proper authority. While at war in Vietnam, standing watch on patrol was a very important position given to me. It carried a huge amount of responsibility. I had to keep vigilant watch over the other soldiers; their lives depended on my watchfulness. I would stay awake in shifts with a few other men called to be on duty and look out into the dark. In the cover of darkness, it was very hard for us to see the enemy approaching. Your eyes and mind play tricks on you in the dark.

Throughout the night, we would be taunted by the Vietnamese soldiers. Through speakers, they would evilly chant, "Marines—tonight you die; we are going to kill you." The enemy was trying to brainwash us and bring fear into our lives. Fear became a factor of war, but we were ready when the enemy came.

We could not fire first because it would give away our position. For the same reason, we could not use the infrared to detect the enemy, which left us with an immense, growing anticipation—waiting, waiting. Then all of a sudden a firefight broke out. Immediately, our bodies felt a sudden rush of adrenaline, and then just as abruptly, the fight was all over. Imagine that!

In Israel's ancient warfare, they would place a man in a high tower, on the wall, and he would watch to see if anyone moved against the city. A watchman's duty was to warn those who were unaware of an oncoming enemy. If he saw the enemy approaching, he would blow the ram's horn as a trumpet and sound the alarm. Then the people would have time to arm themselves for battle and defend the city.

The Prophet Ezekiel was called to be a watchman: *"So you son of man; I have made you a watchman for the house of Israel; therefore you shall hear a word from My mouth and warn them for Me"* (Ezekiel 33:7). In a spiritual sense, as a watchman, he warned the people of Israel not to sin against God. He was responsible to not only hear what God had to say, but to tell the nation of Israel exactly what the Lord had said (Ezekiel 33). Hopefully, this would give them time to turn from their sins and not suffer the Lord's judgment. God has no delight in seeing the wicked perish, as Ezekiel 33:11 tells us: *". . . 'As I live,' says the Lord God, 'I have no pleasure in the death of the wicked, but that the wicked turn from his way and live . . . . '"*

In spiritual warfare we are also called to be watchmen. As believers in Christ, we must have an urgency to share with others the Gospel. This message gives them the way to escape God's judgment coming on the wicked. We have the knowledge of the plan of salvation, so they can be saved.

Ezekiel 33:8-9 explains how each of us will be held accountable in warning others:

> *"When I [God] say to the wicked, 'O wicked man, you shall surely die!' and you do not speak to warn the wicked from his way, that wicked man shall die in his iniquity; but his blood I will require at your hand. Nevertheless if you warn the wicked to turn from his way, and he does not turn from his way, he shall die in his iniquity; but you have delivered your soul."*

It is also very important to keep a watchful eye over our own lives, especially when the enemy attacks us personally. In the Garden of Gethsemane, Jesus told His disciples to *". . . watch with Me."* Afterwards, He went a short distance and prayed, but as He returned, His disciples were all sleeping. Then Jesus warned them again to watch, to stay awake, in case they entered into temptation.

Once again, their flesh, being tired, overtook them and they slept. The enemy was approaching with torches, knives and clubs to arrest Jesus. The hour had come—Christ's time of suffering. When the attack came, His disciples were completely caught off guard, and in the end they all fled (Matthew 26:36-46, 56).

It is crucial for you as a Christian to be disciplined in your watchfulness; you never want to be caught off guard when the enemy approaches. You must learn to stand against him and not run!

IDENTIFY YOUR ENEMIES

One of the most important lessons learned in the military was—always know your surroundings. When ordered on a military operation, we were thoroughly instructed on how to watch out for our enemies, as they would hide—even behind civilians. Our instructors told us, "Do not worry about the ones you can see, be concerned for the ones you cannot see. Those that hide are the ones who will kill you!"

We had learned the basics in boot camp, but because the North Vietnamese looked exactly like the South Vietnamese, the nagging question in the back of everyone's mind was, *Who is my enemy?*

In broad daylight we would go out into the fields where the farmers would be working. We thought the enemy was not around, but the Vietnamese Communists would hide behind these farmers, and all of a sudden, we would be under gun fire. It would turn into a big firefight. Imagine, the enemy would hide in plain sight, and we would be taken by surprise. We had to react quickly and instinctively to defend ourselves.

When I reflect back on the battles in Vietnam, the hardest thing for me to do was to plainly identify and recognize exactly who my real enemies were. Our enemies were clever; they adapted to using different strategies and became very elusive. They were so good at hiding, that our warfare became more like a dangerous cat and mouse game. The Vietnamese would be in a ditch, camouflaged with patches of grass, and, as they stood in the hole, they only had to lift up the patch of grass to be able to snipe at us. Obviously, they could see us, but we couldn't see them.

Our Christian walk is very similar to my experiences in Vietnam. I have learned so much from these encounters in battle. Transferring my knowledge of military warfare and physical battle into the realities of spiritual warfare has given me a real advantage. I clearly understand how to engage the enemy. As a pastor and teacher, watching over people's souls, I feel compelled to equip others to combat the enemy in this on-going battle. Then they can also have spiritual victory in their Christian walks for themselves.

God has taught me to search out the Scriptures in order to identify the enemy. It is a fundamental necessity; then you will be able to automatically counterattack in defense when he strikes. Corrie ten Boom, a survivor of the holocaust, said: "The first step on the way to victory is to recognize the enemy."

In our Christian lives, we will face three main adversaries: our flesh, the world and the devil, along with every one of his demons. These foes will come against us once we have given our lives to the Lord. Therefore, it is important to know each one of these adversaries, and identify their strategies as they attempt to find our weaknesses. We have to recognize them if we want to defeat them. We need to maintain a healthy fear of them; our enemies are very real; they will show us no mercy—they want to kill us!

When it comes down to identifying our enemies, we too can have a hard time. Remember, Satan is never the same in his attacks; he will use many different tactics. He will often hide his plans and remain undetected; therefore, we have to become better acquainted with the different types of strategies Satan uses to destroy our lives. Knowing that you have an enemy who wants to destroy you—be prepared for the battle!

The World

As Christians, the first enemy we should identify is the world. When we are talking about the world, we are speaking about the environment and society around us. As believers, we have been called out of the world. We must live in the world, but we resist the power it has to entice us. From that standpoint, we have to contend with the world in which we live. Satan will use the things of this world to try and take us and our families down. It is a battlefield every single day; every one of us is constantly facing the world as an enemy.

In John 15:19, Jesus tells His disciples: *"If you were of the world, the world would love its own. Yet because you are not of the world, but I chose you out of the world, therefore the world hates you."* Once you became a Christian the world became your enemy! Understand, the things in the world will not edify your life; what the world has to offer will ultimately destroy you.

Look further at what the Bible instructs us about the world—how it is opposed to God and caters to our lusts. In 1 John 2:15-16 it says:

Do not love the world or the things in the world. If anyone loves the world, the love of the Father is not in him. For all

*that is in the world—the lust of the flesh, the lust of the eyes,
and the pride of life—is not of the Father but is of the world.*

First John 2:17 gives us an eternal perspective: *And the
world is passing away, and the lust of it; but he who does the
will of God abides forever.* Seriously, every Christian should
seek and run after the eternal things of the Lord.

The Apostle Paul exhorted the Christians in Rome to pursue
God, not the world. He told them: *And do not be conformed to
this world, but be transformed by the renewing of your mind, that
you may prove what is that good and acceptable and perfect will
of God* (Romans 12:2). The Apostles of Christ knew of Satan's
influence over the things of the world and in their writings,
warned us: *We know that we are of God, and the whole world
lies under the sway of the wicked one* (1 John 5:19).

One of the biggest problems with the world is the one who
rules over it. Satan is the master of this world and dictates the
course of this world. Ephesians 2:2 explains about the path
we once followed: . . . *in which you once walked according to
the course of this world, according to the prince of the power of
the air, the spirit who now works in the sons of disobedience . . .*

When we look around, we can obviously see Satan's hold
on this world. It is amazing to me what people can watch
on television as they go through the channels. There is so
much seduction portrayed, even for all the young children

to see. It is not only acted out on television, but people act inappropriately out in public and no longer have any shame. It is astonishing because there are people who will actually have sex in public, out where children can see them. With the advances in technology, we have seen an increase in online pornography sites. As they are so easily accessible, they have ensnared the hearts and minds of adults and children alike.

Now more than ever, society is confusing adults and children about their sexual identity. Laws are being passed concerning gender rights in the military, public schools and even our local stores. In societies, these changing moral laws will negatively affect our children and grandchildren for years to come.

Drugs and alcohol also continue to be a big problem with our young people today. It is sad that many are killing themselves through drug overdoses and alcohol poisoning. All these ongoing pressures in the world have continued to contribute to the rise of suicide among our youth. Clearly, Satan is using this world to entice our young people into any of these traps. They need the power of Christ to save them!

The Enticement of Egypt

In the Bible, Egypt with its enticements is a type of the world. In the Book of Exodus 14, the children of Israel were in bondage, slaves in Egypt—the world. When God rescued them from their bondage, Moses led them across the Red Sea. God parted the Red Sea and dried up the ground for them to walk over (Exodus 14:21-22). The Red Sea is a picture of water baptism; as they went through, they left the world behind and walked towards a life with God.

What was supposed to be about an 11-day journey into the Promised Land was hindered because of their unbelief (Deuteronomy 1:26-40). Instead, they entered into the wilderness where they spent the next 40 years. They were losing out on the all the blessings God had intended for them, because they did not want to come under full submission to the Lord (Numbers 32:13).

Throughout this time, God provided the people of Israel with godly leadership and divine provision—manna, bread from heaven (Psalm 78:24). But the people still desired Egypt—the world. They did not remember the bondage, but thought things were better under the bondage of Pharaoh than walking freely with the Lord. Look at their evil complaints:

> *And the children of Israel said to them* [Moses and Aaron], *"Oh, that we had died by the hand of the Lord in the land of Egypt, when we sat by the pots of meat and when we ate bread to the full! For you have brought us out into this wilderness to kill this whole assembly with hunger."*
> EXODUS 16:3

And the people thirsted there for water, and the people complained against Moses, and said, "Why is it you have brought us up out of Egypt, to kill us and our children and our livestock with thirst?"

EXODUS 17:3

Now the mixed multitude who were among them yielded to intense craving; so the children of Israel also wept again and said: "Who will give us meat to eat? We remember the fish which we ate freely in Egypt, the cucumbers, the melons, the leeks, the onions, and the garlic; but now our whole being is dried up; there is nothing at all except this manna before our eyes!"

NUMBERS 11:4-6

And all the children of Israel complained against Moses and Aaron, and the whole congregation said to them, "If only we had died in the land of Egypt! Or if only we had died in this wilderness!"

NUMBERS 14:2

As they went through the wilderness, many of the people did not really believe in God, and they longed for the things of the world. They allowed the world to rob them of the blessings God had for them in the Promised Land. Eventually, everyone over the age of 20 died in unbelief. The only two people from that generation to enter into the Promised Land were Joshua and Caleb. They resisted the seduction of the world, trusted God, and chose to follow Him. Joshua would lead the people across the Jordan River on dry ground, into the Promised Land (Joshua 3). In the Promised Land, Israel would face many battles against the heathen nations.

Wandering in the wilderness is a picture of the Christian walking and roaming in worldly pleasure. When people call themselves Christians, but continue to desire the things of the world, they are wandering in the wilderness, missing out on God's perfect plan for their lives.

Just like the children of Israel, unbelief will cause us to forfeit the blessings of God. When we are not willing to submit to the headship of Jesus Christ, we find ourselves in the wilderness. We must choose to walk in the Spirit, being obedient to God by faith.

Crossing the Jordan River is a picture of reckoning the old man to be dead. It represents a full commitment to God, to walk by the Holy Spirit in a life of obedience to God. As you enter Canaan—the Promised Land—it is a life and walk of the believer who is led by the Holy Spirit. Canaan does not represent heaven. Just as Israel faced battles, we also must face many spiritual battles. While we are here on this earth, as a Christian, we battle with the world, our flesh, and the Devil.

The Flesh

The second enemy we have to prepare for is our own flesh, the natural man, who we are without the leading and guiding of the Holy Spirit. Our flesh is something we inherited from Adam, and it is also opposed to God. It is important to remember, Adam was not created in sin with a fleshly nature. When Adam and Eve sinned against God in the Garden of Eden, sin entered into their lives. From that time on, we have all been born in sin with our fleshly nature very much alive, while our spiritual man is dead.

Romans 5:12 tell us: *Therefore, just as through one man sin entered the world, and death through sin, and thus death spread to all men, because all sinned.* Even king David acknowledged this incredible truth: *Behold, I was brought forth in iniquity, and in sin my mother conceived me.* (Psalm 51:5).

Our flesh is dangerous when we yield to its lusts and desires. Satan can come into our lives and tempt us to sin against the Lord using one of his biggest weapons against us—the lust of our own flesh. Seriously, you have to kill the flesh, or it will kill you!

Galatians 5:19-21 identifies the work of the flesh in our lives:

Now the works of the flesh are evident, which are: adultery, fornication, uncleanness, lewdness, idolatry, sorcery, hatred, contentions, jealousies, outbursts of wrath, selfish ambitions, dissensions, heresies, envy, murders, drunkenness, revelries, and the like; of which I tell you beforehand, just as I also told you in time past, that those who practice such things will not inherit the kingdom of God.

Can you identify any of these things in your own life? Recognize the flesh at work and put those things to death. Why? The truth is if you continually yield to the desires of your flesh, and make a practice of sin, you will not go to heaven when you die. Colossians 3:5-6 tells us to put the flesh to death or suffer the consequences:

Therefore put to death your members which are on the earth: fornication, uncleanness, passion, evil desire, and covetousness, which is idolatry. Because of these things the wrath of God is coming upon the sons of disobedience . . .

We can only have victory over our flesh when we put it to death daily. Galatians 5:24-25 tells us how we are to handle our flesh: *And those who are Christ's have crucified the flesh with its passions and desires. If we live in the Spirit, let us also walk in the Spirit.*

Joseph's Temptation

Genesis 39 relates the true story of Joseph, one of Jacob's sons. Joseph was a young man when he was sold into captivity by his brothers and became a slave in Egypt. Potiphar, an officer of Pharaoh, and captain of the guard, bought him from the Ishmaelites, whom his brothers, in jealousy, had sold him as slave. Joseph became very successful as a servant in Potiphar's house, because the Lord was with him and He blessed him tremendously. Potiphar saw his house was being blessed because of Joseph, so he gave him great authority. Joseph was placed in a position of trust; he was given everything in his hands to manage (Genesis 39:1-4).

Notice what is spoken of Joseph in Genesis 39:6: ... *Now Joseph was handsome in form and appearance.* Potiphar's wife, seeing his youthful good looks, began to lust after him. Satan decided to send Joseph a sexual temptation, as he was a child of God, which made him a prime target. He used this woman's flesh to tempt Joseph into yielding to his own fleshly appetites.

In Genesis 39:7-9, the trap was set to cause him to give in to his flesh and sin against God:

> ... *His master's wife cast longing eyes on Joseph, and she said, "Lie with me." But he refused and said to his master's wife, "Look, my master does not know what is with me in the house, and he has committed all that he has to my hand. There is no one greater in this house than I, nor has he kept back anything from me but you, because you are his wife. How then can I do this great wickedness, and sin against God?"*

Potiphar's wife was a brazen woman who tried to seduce Joseph. Remember, he was a young man in the prime of his life, and she wanted him desperately. He could have given in to the lust of his flesh and her desires, but he refused. He submitted to the Spirit and not to his flesh. He remained loyal to his master, but more importantly, Joseph denied his flesh in order to be loyal to the Lord.

In Genesis 39:10, we see she did not give up. His flesh was not tempted only this one time: *So it was, as she spoke to Joseph day by day, that he did not heed her, to lie with her or to be with her.* Finally, she was so frustrated with Joseph, that while no one was looking, she set him up in another attempt to seduce him: . . . *when Joseph went into the house to do his work, and none of the men of the house was inside, that she caught him by his garment, saying, "Lie with me."* (Genesis 39:11-12).

Think about how hard it must have been at this very moment for Joseph to deny his flesh. She was a rich man's wife, a beautiful, well-kept woman. Again, he could have given in to his flesh, and no one would have ever known. I am sure he was tempted to do what she wanted, but he chose not to sin against the Lord. So leaving his garment in her hand, he fled and ran out of the house. In her failure to seduce Joseph, she called out to the men of the house and accused him of attempted rape (Genesis 39:12-15).

Joseph was an honorable man, but Potiphar and his wife were not honorable people. Even though Joseph did the right thing, he was punished because her husband chose to believe her lies. Joseph, an innocent young man, ended up in prison (Genesis 39:20). It seemed as if he denied his flesh for nothing, because he suffered punishment as if he had committed the sin. In reality, God would honor Joseph's faithfulness. Joseph denied his flesh and stayed true to the Lord, and in return, God continued to have His hand upon him and even blessed him while he was in prison: *But the Lord was with Joseph and showed him mercy, and He gave him favor in the sight of the keeper of the prison* (Genesis 39:21).

Through God, Joseph interpreted the dreams of Pharaoh's chief butler and baker who were in prison with him. Therefore, when the Pharaoh had a dream that greatly disturbed him, Egypt's mighty ruler called on Joseph. Through God's providence, Joseph was placed in a position where he was used by God to save Egypt and his family in time of great famine (Genesis 41 and 45).

Joseph is a good example to us of crucifying our flesh when we are tempted. God will always provide a way of escape. It may not be easy, but we always have a choice. It is up to us to deny our flesh and choose to walk in the Spirit, so we can be used by God. In the middle of a great trial, when we choose to be faithful to the Lord, we will be blessed by Him.

The Devil

The third enemy we have is the Devil—Satan. While many people believe Satan is not real, the Bible tells us he is a real being. From the beginning, before Adam and Eve sinned in the Garden of Eden, the world had a great adversary who sought to destroy man, who was created in God's Image. Satan already has the non-believer captive. Without Christ, they are already heading for hell.

Satan comes against Christians. One of the purposes of Satan is to disqualify believers from serving God, but his main goal is to capture and destroy them. We read about his assault against mankind from Genesis to Revelation, where Satan is seen as the fiercest enemy of men. His battle against the believer will continue until the very end of the age.

Character of Satan

If we are going to withstand the wiles of Satan, we have to know him and his character. Unlike the way Satan is characterized in cartoons and movies, he is not the typical, twisted creature with horns, a tail and a pitchfork. As we go through the Bible and look at the many times he is addressed, his character is revealed by his names and by his actions.

First Peter 5:8 warns us that Satan is as a roaring lion: *Be sober, be vigilant; because your adversary the devil walks about like a roaring lion, seeking whom he may devour.* Like a lion, he stalks all believers, waiting for the moment when he can leap. He looks for weak Christians, those who are not in God's Word or in prayer so he can attack them and bring them down. He also pursues the mature Christian deviously, strategizing to devour them. That is why we must be in the word and prayer to be ready for an attack, because Satan never stops prowling. He is always on the hunt.

Jesus referred to Satan as a thief: The *thief does not come except to steal, and to kill, and to destroy . . .* (John 10:10). He also revealed Satan to be a murderer and a liar:

> *You* [Pharisees] *are of your father the devil, and the desires of your father you want to do. He was a murderer from the beginning, and does not stand in the truth, because there is no truth in him. When he speaks a lie, he speaks from his own resources, for he is a liar and the father of it.*
>
> JOHN 8:44

Satan has another title; it was given to him by the religious leaders in Jesus' day. They wrongly identified Jesus' miracles with demonic power: *Now when the Pharisees heard it they said, "This fellow does not cast out demons except by Beelzebub,* [Beelzebub in the Greek means "dung-god"] *the ruler of the demons"* (Matthew 12:24).

In Mark 5:1-20, Jesus met a man who was demon possessed. He lived among the tombs and had abnormal strength. Under demonic influence, he would often cry out and cut himself with stones. When people are possessed by demons, they become very strong and often hurt themselves. Satan's demons will try to destroy a person and even influence them to commit suicide. Jesus addressed the demon that had the man in torment: *"Come out of the man, unclean spirit!" Then He asked him, "What is your name?" And he answered, saying, "My name is Legion; for we are many"* (Mark 5:8-9).

In the Greek, the word *Legion* refers to a Roman regiment. It is further described as a body of soldiers whose number differed, and in the time of Augustus seems to have consisted of 6,826 men or 6100 foot soldiers and 726 horsemen. One man was possessed by thousands of demons—can you believe that?

The Apostle John unveils the truth of how Satan strategizes against believers. In Revelation 12:10, he gives us a look into the future, where Satan is called the accuser of the brethren. This Scripture reveals how he is still operating today:

Then I heard a loud voice saying in heaven, "Now salvation, and strength, and the kingdom of our God, and the power of His Christ have come, for the accuser of our brethren, who accused them [Saints] *before our God day and night, has been cast down."*

After looking at the character of Satan, it is easy to get scared. He seems undefeatable. It is true he is a powerful being. You have no need to fear Satan; if you are a child of God all you have to do is call upon the Lord. Paul the Apostle said it perfectly: *What then shall we say to these things? If God is for us, who can be against us?* (Romans 8:31). Honestly, if God is for us, we should not fear Satan. At the end of the age, God will deal with Satan, the deceiver: *The devil, who deceived them* [the nations] *was cast into the lake of fire and brimstone . . .* where he *will be tormented day and night forever and ever* (Revelation 20:10).

Satan Limited by God

When we talk about spiritual warfare, it is so important to keep these things in mind; God is omnipotent—all-powerful. He is also omniscient—all knowing, and omnipresent—present everywhere at one time. Satan is not more powerful than God or equal in power to Him. He is very limited and has none of these attributes. Remember, God created Satan as a great Cherub, but because of pride and rebellion, he became Satan. He knows he cannot defeat God; so instead, he pursues man to destroy him, who was created in the image of God. Satan gets great delight when he causes man to embrace sin.

Knowing Satan is defenseless against the Lord, we can hold onto all the words of Psalm 121. We can look to the heavens, to the Lord, knowing where our help comes from, Creator of heaven and earth. He never sleeps, but He watches over us. He is our keeper—preserving our souls from evil.

Job's Intense Testing

The Book of Job is one of the oldest books in the Bible. It tells the story of Job, a godly man who went through a tremendous spiritual battle. From the very first chapter, Satan's plan is revealed, as he sought permission from the Lord to destroy Job's life. As we study the story of Job, we shall see the limited power of Satan, while displaying the great power and might of the Lord. These important insights will help us to better understand an unseen, spiritual warfare, from behind the scenes.

Job was a man who loved God and remained in constant, intimate communion with Him. He was very prosperous, and he knew God had blessed him. Job's life was one of great integrity. He knew what was righteous and unrighteous before God, and he did no evil. Job 1:1 introduces him:

There was a man in the land of Uz, whose name was Job; and that man was blameless and upright, and one who feared God and shunned evil. He had great possessions: . . . seven thousand sheep, three thousand camels, five hundred yoke of oxen, five hundred female donkeys, and a very large household, so that this man was the greatest of all the people of the East.

JOB 1:2-3

Job, as a husband and father, was the spiritual leader of his home. He watched over his very large family. Job was blessed with seven sons and three daughters, who he loved greatly. He even took responsibility for their spiritual well-being. Job got up early in the morning and prayed for his entire family and gave sacrifices to consecrate his home: ... *he would rise early in the morning and offer burnt offerings according to the number of them all. For Job said, "It may be that my sons have sinned and cursed God in their hearts." Thus Job did regularly* (Job 1:5).

Notice, Job prayed regularly, not just once in a while. He was faithfully committed to serving the Lord and his family. As a man who walked closely with the Lord, he was an enemy to Satan, who was not happy with the faithfulness of Job. He singled Job out, asking the Lord's permission to test him. Job 1:6-7 gives us a detailed look of what was happening behind the scenes of Job's life: *Now there was a day when the sons of God came to present themselves before the Lord, and Satan also came among them. And the Lord said to Satan, "From where do you come?"*

Imagine, Satan had to check in with God; he stood before Him—the One who ultimately gave him consent to do anything. The term, *sons of God*, in the Old Testament, is used in reference to angels—those who came and stood before God. Satan also came before the throne of God to accuse Job. When they were all assembled, God inquired of Satan: *"From where do you come?"* Now, many would say this is a mistake in the Word of God, because God did not know where Satan was, when God knows everything. This is not an error. God knew exactly where Satan had been and what was happening the whole time, because Satan works under God's authority. Although God knew, the other angels did not know what was happening. So the conversation continued: *So Satan answered the Lord and said, "From going to and fro on the earth, and from walking back and forth on it"* (Job 1:7).

God knows Satan's tactics and knew exactly why Satan was roaming the earth, so He asked him: *Then the Lord said to Satan, "Have you considered My servant Job, that there is none like him on the earth, a blameless and upright man, one who fears God and shuns evil?"* (Job 1:8).

Notice the integrity of Job. God knew Job's heart toward Him, and allowed Satan to test Job:

So Satan answered the Lord and said, "Does Job fear God for nothing? Have You not made a hedge around him, around his household, and around all that he has on every side? You have blessed the work of his hands, and his possessions have increased in the land. But now, stretch out Your hand and touch all that he has, and he will surely curse You to Your face!"
JOB 1:9-11

In response, God gave Satan permission to tempt Job, but he could not take his life. Job would be preserved. God stayed in complete control: *And the Lord said to Satan, "Behold, all that he has is in your power; only do not lay a hand on his person."* God knew Job loved Him, and He knew he would withstand the devil's attacks. Satan did not waste any time; he went out after Job and all he possessed: *So Satan went out from the presence of the Lord* (Job 1:12).

In one day, Satan would take everything from Job. Satan thought he could get Job to turn against God if he took away his family and all his worldly possessions. The character of Job was under attack. His true nature would be revealed in this great trial. Job 1:13-19 tells us how this dreadful day began:

Now there was a day when his sons and daughters were eating and drinking wine in their oldest brother's house; and a messenger came to Job and said, "The oxen were plowing and the donkeys feeding beside them, when the Sabeans raided them and took them away—indeed they have killed the servants with the edge of the sword; and I alone have escaped to tell you!" While he was still speaking, another also came and said, "The fire of God fell from heaven and burned up the sheep and the servants, and consumed them; and I alone have escaped to tell you!" While he was still speaking, another also came and said, "The Chaldeans formed three bands, raided the camels and took them away, yes, and killed the servants with the edge of the sword; and I alone have escaped to tell you!" While he was still speaking, another also came and said, "Your sons and daughters were eating and drinking wine in their oldest brother's house, and suddenly a great wind came from across the wilderness and struck the four corners of the house, and it fell on the young people, and they are dead; and I alone have escaped to tell you!"

Satan must have sat back and waited to see if Job would turn against God. He was so sure he had done enough to make Job curse God. But look at Job's response:

Then Job arose, tore his robe, and shaved his head; and he fell to the ground and worshiped. And he said: "Naked I came from my mother's womb, and naked shall I return there. The Lord gave, and the Lord has taken away; blessed be the name of the Lord." In all this Job did not sin nor charge God with wrong.

JOB 1:20-22

After Satan took everything from him, Job did not curse God, or sin against Him foolishly. He not only worshiped the Lord, but he thanked Him for everything He had given to him. Job had an eternal perspective and recognized the preeminence of the Lord. He knew his possessions, even his sons and daughters, belonged to God. They were the Lord's and He could take them away, at any time.

Satan went on to tempt and try Job in even greater ways, but he never turned against the Lord. Job remained faithful because he knew the character of God. Job was a man of God, armed in full spiritual armor, ready to withstand the attacks of the enemy.

Today and every day, Satan still stands before the throne of God, accusing Christians of evil and seeks our destruction. In Revelation 12:10, Satan is named the *Accuser of our Brethren*. In the future he will be cast down. But this Scripture describes his present activity, which is to accuse the believer before our God day and night. But God can divinely protect you, and He will not allow Satan to kill you. You may ask yourself, "How much would God allow Satan to tempt me?" It is important to understand, the Lord is not going to allow the Devil to do anything more to you than you can handle. He will permit you to be tempted but He will always provide a way out (1 Corinthians 10:13).

During times of testing, may we be like Job who never accused God falsely. We need to continue to be faithful to Him, no matter what He gives and takes away from us. Whatever our circumstances, let us worship God as we stand in His presence. We must remember Satan comes in seasons; he never gives up. He always comes back stronger, even more prepared than the time before. Like Job, are we spiritually prepared—fully armed, to face our adversary?

Demons

Satan does not work alone; he has a great army he uses against us—his demons. Remember, when Satan was cast out of heaven, he took one-third of the angels with him. We cannot even see them, but they are present. Just as Satan is very dangerous and powerful, his demons are likewise. Demons, as Satan's workers, have evil intentions towards mankind. Their main work is causing Christians to fall into sin. They are able to harass believers and literally possess non-believers, in order to have a body. Mary Magdalene, who followed Jesus, had been such a woman: *and certain women who had been healed of evil spirits and infirmities—Mary called Magdalene, out of whom had come seven demons* (Luke 8:2).

These demonic enemies are described by Paul the Apostle in Ephesians 6:12: *For we do not wrestle against flesh and blood, but against principalities, against powers, against the rulers of the darkness of this age, against spiritual hosts of wickedness in the heavenly places.* Our warfare is against organized ranks of fallen angels, demonic beings with superhuman strength, world rulers governing over hosts of fallen angels.

We have learned, Satan, unlike God, cannot know everything and be everywhere; he is limited. But this is why he uses his vast number of messengers to collect useful information about us. Just as a military unit has men to go out and do reconnaissance on their enemy, Satan has his demons go out to study us, and they come back to report to him. That is why Satan knows so much concerning us. Yet, we do not have to live in fear of demons, but we must be wise in knowing our enemies, or we will be trapped by them.

Imagine, there is a battle going on between God's angelic hosts and the army of Satan's wicked angelic beings, who are fighting for the souls of mankind. This unseen battle was revealed by the angel Gabriel, after Daniel prayed to God in Daniel 10:12-13:

> *Then he said to me, "Do not fear, Daniel, for from the first day that you set your heart to understand, and to humble yourself before your God, your words were heard; and I have come because of your words. But the prince of the kingdom of Persia* [Satan] *withstood me twenty-one days; and behold, Michael* [the archangel]*, one of the chief princes, came to help me, for I had been left alone there with the kings of Persia."*

Daniel had been praying three times a day for three long weeks. God heard Daniel the first time and had an answer for him, but it took the angel Gabriel, three weeks to get to Daniel, because Satan and his demons had been trying to stop him. There had been a great angelic battle. Spiritual warfare not only took place with the Old Testament saints; but has never ceased and continues to today. That is how much Satan hates you and me. He battles the powerful angels of God to defeat us. There are angels and demons battling daily for our lives—amazing!

While God's angels are fighting, what to us is an unseen spiritual battle for our souls, we too need to fight, because we are living in this world in a body that is temporal—not eternal.

In talking about the Christian life and the battle we are in, I am reminded of a class I once took on all the world religions. The professor said demon activity would become more intense in the last days before Jesus Christ comes. We can see that demonic activity is on the rise in America, but in other parts of the world there is great oppression and demon activity. This very much agrees with what Paul said in 1 Timothy 4:1-2:

> *Now the Spirit expressly says that in latter times some will depart from the faith, giving heed to deceiving spirits and doctrines of demons, speaking lies in hypocrisy, having their own conscience seared with a hot iron . . .*

The most important thing Christians have to remember about demons is that they cannot possess a true Christian. Once you are filled with the Holy Spirit, Satan and his demons cannot enter in. However, they can harass, oppress and try to deceive you. Satan will even try, through oppression, to influence a person to commit suicide. Understand, demons are liars and deceivers, transforming themselves into angels of light, just like their master, Satan.

Paul the Apostle warned the believers concerning Satan and his demons' tactics in 2 Corinthians 11:13-15:

> *For such are false apostles, deceitful workers, transforming themselves into apostles of Christ. And no wonder! For Satan himself transforms himself into an angel of light. Therefore*

it is no great thing if his ministers also transform themselves into ministers of righteousness, whose end will be according to their works.

As we look at the spiritual battles we experience as Christians, we have to understand, the attacks from the enemy are not new. In the beginning, man and woman were created perfect, but still temptation came into the Garden of Eden, and the battle began between good and evil—between the things of God and Satan. As we go through the Bible, we can see how the men and women who followed and loved the Lord experienced great trials and tribulations. They were in tremendous warfare.

Unfortunately, from the many stories we have gone through, we know Satan is going to use our flesh and the world to try to cause us to sin. The enemy will use these for our destruction. Remember, Satan and his demons have one goal, to destroy us, and if we allow it, our own flesh and the world around us will be his greatest weapons of destruction. As followers of Christ we do not have to be discouraged. Jesus said: . . . *I have come that they may have life, and that they may have it more abundantly* (John 10:10). That is the purpose of His coming—to save and help you, it is through Christ that we can be victorious; He can give us the victory!

Chapter 3

CASUALTIES IN WARFARE

*This charge I commit to you, son Timothy, according
to the prophecies previously made concerning you, that
by them you may wage the good warfare, having faith and
a good conscience, which some having rejected, concerning
the faith have suffered shipwreck . . .*
1 TIMOTHY 1:18, 19

FIRST CASUALTIES

In war, you will always have casualties—the wounded
and the killed. The names of over 58,000 men, including eight
women, POWs, MIAs and others are inscribed on the Vietnam
Wall. It is a silent, grim reminder of those who gave their lives
willingly for our American freedom.

In Vietnam, to avoid becoming a casualty, we needed to
strictly adhere to the training we were given. In boot camp,

our instructors told us that our helmets needed to be worn at all times. I can remember some of the first casualties were young men who thoughtlessly took off their helmets. It was a fatal mistake, and it cost them their lives.

At camp, our Unit, Alpha 1/7, felt safe, and we would casually talk to each other about our families—knowing, in the back of our minds that when we were called out on an operation, someone would return as a wounded or maimed soldier, or he would become a fatality. Many soldiers were injured or killed unexpectedly in warfare. Booby traps, usually a grenade in a ditch with a trip wire, were not easy to detect; many times our men would walk right into the enemy's traps.

On one occasion, we believed our surroundings were completely secure—there was a village on one side, and on the other side, a gate. My friend Pete Silva, who was walking point, undertook the first and most dangerous lead position. He was very familiar with the enemies' tactics. Since usually the VC would trap the doors and gates with hand-grenades or a bouncing-betty, he had decided to jump over the gate instead of next to it. Horrifically, he hit a trip wire; he had stepped on a booby trap and went flying. When Pete landed, shards of shrapnel from the blast had blown off both his legs, one went to the right and the other one to the left—horrible. I could hear him screaming and crying. We were all in shock; the trap was unexpected. Our enemies had become smart; as we had anticipated their moves, they had decided to change their battle tactics.

Although dazed, I began to look around—Pete was on the ground, face down. I had been right behind him and my back was now filled with shrapnel. If it had not been for the bulletproof vest I was wearing, I would have been a dead man—the shrapnel would have pierced through to my lungs. We called for MEDEVAC, and waited two long hours together for the helicopter. When it finally arrived, I carried Pete on my back, picking up his legs and entering safely into the helicopter. I loved him and wanted to see the doctors help him.

Another sad tragedy for me to watch in Vietnam was the men who decided to have sex with the local prostitutes. They had no idea what they were getting themselves in to; there would be serious consequences. These young men found out later they had contracted a deadly venereal disease—black syphilis. There is no known cure; it is a terminal disease. They never came back home; they were done—that was the end of that. Through submitting to the desires of their flesh, they became part of the growing numbers of men added to the list of casualties of war.

Solomon's Warning

King Solomon wrote about the temptations of the whorish woman in the Book of Proverbs. He was a man well acquainted with the lusts of the flesh and gave in to its desires: . . . *he had seven hundred wives, princesses, and three hundred concubines;*

and his wives turned away his heart (1 Kings 11:3). He was no longer loyal to the Lord.

In Solomon's old age, he was able to look back and clearly see the errors of his ways. In his life, he had given in to the lusts of his flesh, which caused him to move further away from the Lord. He had walked in his flesh and not in the Spirit; God could not use him to the fullest. I believe with all my heart, this is what prompted him to write the proverbs about the crafty harlot.

Solomon warned men to beware of the women he saw on the streets, those trying to entice gullible, young men to engage in illicit sex. From his words, it seems as if Solomon sat in his house as he wrote:

> *For at the window of my house I looked through my lattice, and saw among the simple, I perceived among the youths, a young man devoid of understanding, passing along the street near her corner; and he took the path to her house in the twilight, in the evening, in the black and dark night. And there a woman met him, with the attire of a harlot, and a crafty heart.*
>
> PROVERBS 7:6-10

Solomon saw this crafty woman on the streets, dressed seductively, as she tried to lure foolish men into her house. She not only dressed to seduce him, but with her actions, she appealed to the lust of his flesh. Proverbs 7:11-18 fully describes her:

She was loud and rebellious, her feet would not stay at home. At times she was outside, at times in the open square, lurking at every corner. So she caught him and kissed him; with an impudent face she said to him: "I have peace offerings with me; today I have paid my vows. So I came out to meet you, diligently to seek your face, and I have found you. I have spread my bed with tapestry, colored coverings of Egyptian linen. I have perfumed my bed with myrrh, aloes, and cinnamon. Come, let us take our fill of love until morning; let us delight ourselves with love."

The harlot had met this young man on the street and grabbed him to kiss him. Her seductive words had him filled with lust. Attempting to satisfy his aroused passions, she invited him to her home to have sex. Her bed was prepared, and he was made to believe she had done it all for him. But she was a whorish woman, seeking any young, foolish man.

Imagine, she was not just trying to lure this young man to fornicate with her, she was causing him to commit adultery, for she was a married woman. Her husband had gone out on business and she decided to seduce some young man while he was gone: *"For my husband is not at home; he has gone on a long journey; he has taken a bag of money with him, and will come home on the appointed day"* (Proverbs 7:19-20). If this woman's husband found out, this young man was a dead man!

Solomon watched the young man give in to temptation:

With her enticing speech she caused him to yield, with her flattering lips she seduced him. Immediately he went after her, as an ox goes to the slaughter, or as a fool to the correction of the stocks, till an arrow struck his liver. As a bird hastens to the snare, he did not know it would cost his life.

PROVERBS 7:21-23

He went with the crafty woman, but he did not know he was being led to the slaughter. Yielding to his flesh cost him his physical life; he may have caught a venereal disease. Not only did this young man lose his physical life, but it cost him his spiritual life too.

At the end of the proverb, Solomon issues a strong warning. He tells us the final end for those who indulge with prostitutes: *Her house is the way to hell, descending to the chambers of death* (Proverbs 7:27). In this chapter, we saw a young man who became a casualty because he was not able to control his flesh—death and hell were the terrifying results.

Just like Solomon who watched these young men go to houses of harlotry, I was reminded of the young soldiers who went into these same types of harlots. They were in warfare against their enemy, fighting the Vietnamese; but they did not realize that by satisfying their flesh with these women, they would pay a high price physically. It is only through Christ that Christians can avoid the traps set by the enemy to entice their flesh. We need to pay attention to God's instructions in His Word. Then we will not be listed among the first casualties or fatalities in spiritual warfare.

The Parable of the Sower

As a pastor, you can imagine how I get really excited when people come forward at an altar call to get saved. But I also know the spiritual battle has just begun for them. It is important for those who have become truly born again in Christ to immediately get into a Bible teaching church. They need to start reading the Word of God the minute they get saved and begin to speak to the Lord in prayer. Otherwise, they will become casualties. They will fall victim to the tactics of our enemies—the flesh, the world and Satan.

There are many casualties in the body of Christ; it is so sad. I often see an empty seat in church where a familiar person used to sit. I ask myself, "Where are they?" "How did the enemy get to them?"

I believe the Parable of the Sower, in Mark 4 explains to us what happens to these people. It is one of the most important parables that Jesus ever preached to the multitudes. The theme of the whole chapter is *"He who has ears to hear, let him hear!"* One thing that I feel and I see constantly is that we do not hear what God is saying—we do not give an ear to the things of the Lord. It is a big problem among believers today; we kind of listen, but not wholeheartedly to the proclamation God is making to our hearts.

As Jesus was moving in a circuit around the Sea of Galilee, He began to teach the Parable of the Sower: *And again He began to teach by the sea. And a great multitude was gathered to Him, so that He got into a boat and sat in it on the sea; and the whole multitude was on the land facing the sea* (Mark 4:1).

Notice, within the first verse we see the importance of the teaching of God's Word. What is interesting is that the whole multitude of people in the previous chapter were constantly surrounding and touching Him. It got to the point where Jesus could not move freely around any longer— He had become so popular. But the multitudes were only coming looking for a meal or to be touched by Jesus so they could be physically, emotionally or spiritually healed—not necessarily to hear His words.

Jesus got to the point where He needed space, and so He chose to get into a little boat and go offshore. He took the role of their Teacher. The people remained standing and He, as their Teacher, would be sitting—this was the Jewish custom in Israel. A teacher would stand to read the Scriptures, but they sat when they expounded on the text (Nehemiah 8:1-6; Matthew 23:2).

Notice how Jesus taught the people: *Then He taught them many things by parables...* (Mark 4:2). Jesus constantly used parables, especially in the Gospel of Matthew, here in Mark 4, and in Luke's Gospel. Jesus spoke about 30 parables—they were extremely important. Now, each parable was given in such a way that the people would be able to understand what Jesus taught. When defining a parable, it was given in the form of a story, as an illustration, for people to understand a truth of God. Whenever Jesus would use stories or parables, He would always identify Himself with the land Israel or the people, in whatever was common to their way of life—but it was always by association. Israel was a land to cultivate crops, such as wheat; many of the people were farmers.

The Parable of the Sower would relate to the people as farmers. Jesus would use the familiarity of tilling and sowing seed to get across the message of listening to the Word of God. Within the parable, you get a picture of the land; it had been cleared of rocks, tilled, watered and fertilized. The farmer, who is the sower in the field, is throwing out the seed. The sower is a beautiful picture or type of Jesus Christ, and the seed is the type of the Word of God, as the Word is being given out to the people.

Associating the parable with us today, there are still four types of hearers. I recommend that you pay close attention and see where you fit among the four illustrations Jesus will now give to us in the Parable of the Sower:

> *"Listen! Behold, a sower went out to sow. And it happened, as he sowed, that some seed fell by the wayside; and the birds of the air came and devoured it. Some fell on stony ground, where it did not have much earth; and immediately it sprang up because it had no depth of earth. But when the sun was up it was scorched, and because it had no root it withered away. And some seed fell among thorns; and the thorns grew up and choked it, and it yielded no crop. But other seed fell on good ground and yielded a crop that sprang up,* increased *and produced: some thirtyfold, some sixty, and some a hundred."*
>
> MARK 4:3-8

Jesus, in His teaching, establishes the plan of salvation and the way into the kingdom of God. Literally, what He is teaching is that you can find four different types of people that are sitting in churches and elsewhere around the world.

The first group He speaks about is those that fell by the wayside. The birds came by and ate the seeds. In Scripture, birds can represent evil and can be a type of Satan; they signify him coming to rob the Word of God from their hearts—Satan snatches the seed away.

The second group is those on the stony ground. These people are emotional hearers who at first are happy to hear God's Word, but withdraw back into the world when trials and persecution arise. The Word of God never took root in their hearts, and it withered and died.

Third, Jesus addresses another group of people, where the Word of God becomes overcome by the cares and desires of this world.

Fourth, Jesus ends the parable by identifying true Christians, those who are fruitful. The Lord begins using them to win others to Christ.

Now, after the parable, Jesus exhorted the people: *And He said to them, "He who has ears to hear, let him hear!"* (Mark 4:9). In this exhortation, He gave an invitation to pay attention to the "Parable of the Sower" and to listen carefully so they can recognize where they fit in the parable. You have to examine your life and ask, "What kind of hearer describes my life?" Then in verses 10-12, Jesus gave us the purpose for the parable:

> *But when He was alone, those around Him with the twelve asked Him about the parable. And He said to them, "To you it has been given to know the mystery of the kingdom of God; but to those who are outside, all things come in parables, so that 'Seeing they may see and not perceive, and hearing they may hear and not understand; lest they should turn, and their sins be forgiven them.' "*

In the world, a mystery is something that is covered and hidden—it is a secret, but not so in the Bible. God revealed to His disciples what the kingdom of God was all about. In the Old Testament, it was a secret, but not so in the New Testament.

When Jesus Christ came, the mystery of the kingdom of God was fully revealed to them. Now it can be fully understood to anyone who wants to be saved.

Jesus also spoke about the non-believers, those who are *outside*, such as the Pharisees, Sadducees and the Scribes—the spiritual leaders of that time who were rejecting Him. These men had hardened hearts and were outside of the kingdom of God (Isaiah 6:9-10, 43:8; Jeremiah 5:25).

Now many people among the multitudes did not listen to what Jesus was saying concerning the Word of God. I have found that there are people who will come to church one time, for three to six months or even for years, and yet they were never born again of the Holy Spirit—they became religious people. It is amazing to me, because I have seen and known people at Calvary Chapel who have sat and listened to the teaching of God's Word for three years when I found out they never really walked with God. I asked myself, *What in the world happened?* Then I had to go back to the Parable of the Sower for the answer. These people never, ever gave place to the Word of God in their hearts. They were never obedient or submissive to God.

You see, the only people in the Parable of the Sower who actually brought forth results of thirty, sixty and a hundred fold, were those who opened up their hearts and responded to the Word of God. They listened to the Word of God, allowed the Seed that was sown in their hearts to be watered, then the Word of God took root in their lives, and they brought forth the fruit—the others had no fruit at all.

You have to honestly ask yourself, "Am I bringing forth fruit in my life?" The greatest evidence of fruit in our lives is the love of Christ. The fruit of the Spirit is love (Galatians 5:22). Do you have love in your hearts for others around you? Will you share with them the Gospel of Jesus Christ?

What I love about this parable is that we do not have a responsibility to convert people, but we do have the duty to share His Word with others.

SATAN ASSAULTS THE SAINTS

Satan Sifts Peter

Jesus was eating the Last Supper with His disciples before Judas betrayed him. The Lord was explaining about His kingdom when He turned to Peter and said: *". . . Simon, Simon! Indeed, Satan has asked for you, that he may sift you as wheat."* Notice, after that statement, Jesus encouraged Peter: *"But I have prayed for you, that your faith should not fail; and when you have returned to Me, strengthen your brethren."* Peter impulsively and zealously responded to Jesus: *"Lord, I am ready to go with You, both to prison and to death."* As Jesus is omniscient—all-knowing—He told Peter what would happen in his future: *"I tell you, Peter, the rooster shall not crow this day before you will deny three times that you know Me"* (Luke 22:31-34). It would not be long before Jesus' words would come to pass.

Before Peter denied the Lord, there were obvious steps he took that caused him to become, for a time, a casualty. His first step backwards was his self-confidence; he trusted in himself—not God. He said to Jesus: *"Even if all are made to stumble because of You, I will never be made to stumble"* (Matthew 26:33).

In his second step backward, Peter failed to pray; he slept and was unprepared to stand against the enemy:

Then He [Jesus] *came to the disciples and found them sleeping, and said to Peter, "What! Could you not watch with Me one hour? Watch and pray, lest you enter into temptation. The spirit indeed is willing, but the flesh is weak."*
                                                                          MATTHEW 26:40-41

The word *watch* means "to be sleepless, to be awake, attentive and vigilant." The disciples should have been in prayer so they would not have entered into temptation, just as Jesus was with the Father, fervently in prayer—but they slept. The spirit was willing to stay awake and pray, but they gave in to their flesh and fell asleep.

Jesus left to pray, not once, but two more times:

Again, a second time, He went away and prayed, saying, "O My Father, if this cup cannot pass away from Me unless I drink it, Your will be done." And He came and found them asleep again, for their eyes were heavy. So He left them, went away again, and prayed the third time, saying the same words. Then He came to His disciples and said to them, "Are you still sleeping and resting? Behold, the hour is at hand, and the Son of Man is being betrayed into the hands of sinners. Rise, let us be going. See, My betrayer is at hand."

MATTHEW 26:42-46

His disciples were completely without power. They had slept and not spent time in prayer. They would face a great trial as the religious leaders and guards came to take Jesus, and they were not prepared. Even though Jesus warned Peter that he would deny Him, he did not listen to Jesus. He thought he was so strong, but without spending time with God in prayer, he failed in his trial.

Jesus' warning to Peter is a great warning to every Christian. Martin Luther understood this warning when he said, "To be a Christian without prayer is just as impossible as to be alive without breathing." Prayer is like oxygen. We need it. We cannot live without it. We will not have victory over the trials and temptations, and yet, many people are living without it.

Peter's third step backward was *following afar off*—distanced from his Master. After Jesus' betrayal and arrest . . . *Peter followed Him at a distance to the high priest's courtyard. And he went in and sat with the servants to see the end* (Matthew 26:58).

Peter's fourth step led him to denial, leaving him with no strength or power and he denied the Lord: . . . *And a little later those who stood by came up and said to Peter, "Surely you also are one* of them, for your speech betrays you." *Then he began to curse and swear, saying, "I do not know the Man!" Immediately a rooster crowed* (Matthew 26:73-74).

Peter's final step was in the right direction. Peter realized what he had done, remembered what Jesus had said and he immediately repented (Matthew 26:75).

When Christ resurrected, He made breakfast and met Peter on the beach. After they had both eaten, Jesus asked Peter,

"Simon, son of Jonah, do you love Me more than these?"

He said to Him, "Yes, Lord; You know that I love You."

He said to him, "Feed My lambs." He said to him again a second time, "Simon, son of Jonah, do you love Me?"

He said to Him, "Yes, Lord; You know that I love You."

He said to him, "Tend My sheep." He said to him the third time, "Simon, son of Jonah, do you love Me?" Peter was grieved because He said to him the third time, "Do you love Me?"

And he said to Him, "Lord, You know all things; You know that I love You."

Jesus said to him, "Feed My sheep."

JOHN 21:15-17

Peter was a broken man. He had become a casualty in spiritual warfare, but through Christ, he was brought back into fellowship with Him. Then, Jesus addressed Peter, He foretold him of his death and how he would glorify God (John 21:18). Afterwards, the Lord repeated to him the same two, simple words He spoke when they had first met, *"Follow Me"* (John 21:19). Why? Jesus told Peter, who was a fisherman by profession, that He would make him a fisher of men (Matthew 4:19). Jesus renewed Peter's call and commissioned him; restoring his life, fully and completely.

Then on the Day of Pentecost, Peter received the Holy Spirit. At that time, he was empowered to preach the Gospel, and about three thousand souls were added to the Church (Acts 2:14-41).

Looking back over Peter's life, do you find yourself in a place like he was? Can you recognize how far you have drifted away from your relationship with Christ? Backsliding does not happen overnight; these backward steps can be subtle.

On one occasion, I left my keys with a lifeguard at the lifeguard tower closest to my car and went surfing. When I returned to collect my keys at the tower, they were gone! The lifeguard helped me look for them—were they lost in the sand? I searched around for my car—nowhere to be found. As I began to walk farther along the beach, I found my car. Unknowingly, as I surfed, I had drifted away from my car and the original lifeguard tower. Imagine that!

At times, Christians do not even realize how far they have drifted from the truth. They become undisciplined in their devotional time and gradually drift away going to church services regularly. Instead, they go to the movies, baseball games or other sports on Sundays. Before they know it, they start hanging around with non-Christian friends. Slowly but surely, the enemy gains a foothold in their lives, and they become backslidden, a casualty of spiritual warfare. I see it all the time.

If you have tripped, fallen or slowly drifted away from the Lord, as a Christian, then allow Christ to work in your life through sincere repentance. In your brokenness, do not let the enemy lie and convince you that you have gone too far—causing you to believe that you can never return to the Lord. The enemy will whisper lies, telling you that your sins are too great. Has the cross of Christ become of no effect in your life? I plead with you—return back to the Lord; it is never too late. Read 1 John 1:9, 10:

If we confess our sins, He is faithful and just to forgive us our sins and to cleanse us from all unrighteousness. If we say that we have not sinned, we make Him a liar, and His word is not in us.

Through repentance, Jesus will forgive you and restore your life, fully and completely.

Prisoner of War

Being taken as a prisoner of war is one of the worst things that could happen to an American soldier. As Marines, my unit formed a tight knit bond with one another. Our close, bonded unit vowed we would never be taken captive, because the enemy was brutal; they tortured soldiers and mutilated them in death. Even if we had to kill each other, we promised one another we would never get taken by the Vietnamese soldiers.

The Apostle Paul addressed himself as a prisoner: . . . *I, Paul, the prisoner of Christ Jesus . . .* (Ephesians 3:1). Even though he had entered a spiritual battle that had cost him his freedom, he never let being in prison stop him from sharing the Gospel. Paul knew that, even from his prison cell, his trials were for the furtherance of the Gospel:

But I want you to know, brethren, that the things which happened to me have actually turned out for the furtherance of the Gospel, so that it has become evident to the whole palace guard, and to all the rest, that my chains are in

Christ; and most of the brethren in the Lord, having become confident by my chains, are much more bold to speak the word without fear.

PHILIPPIANS 1:12-14

In the end, according to Christian tradition, Paul was martyred by Nero. He gave his life for the sake of the Gospel. Paul always had an eternal perspective—he never feared death. He said in life: *For to me, to live is Christ, and to die is gain* (Philippians 1:21). Think of that, instantly, the moment Paul died, he was present before the Lord!

Have you noticed more and more Christians are being persecuted for their faith worldwide? There are radical Muslim groups—terrorists that are targeting Christian men, women and children. They are imprisoning, torturing, burning, beheading and crucifying them. Recently, in some countries in the Middle East, there have been mass genocides among Christian communities. Even Christians in America have suffered tremendously because of the brutal attacks on them. Our duty is to pray for the persecutors and to never forget the persecuted believers in Christ, across the world. Hebrews 13:3 tells us*: Remember the prisoners as if chained with them—those who are mistreated—since you yourselves are in the body also.*

AWOL

What does AWOL mean? It means, Absent Without Leave—a soldier absent from the armed forces without permission. One who, out of fear, runs and does not stand with his unit. He hightails it out of danger and leaves his men. This is considered cowardice, and it is hated by all the other soldiers; our very lives depend on each other, and there needs to be loyalty among us.

On this one occasion, when we were way out from our base, we headed straight into an ambush and we were hit really hard. There was one guy in our platoon that we could not find. What happened? He ran all the way back to our base and left us there. When I returned, I was so mad, I took my rifle and whipped him; I was almost going to shoot him. In the end, we told our officers to get him out of our platoon.

How can you trust someone like that? He almost cost us our lives! I did not want to be with traitors or weak people in war. When it comes to spiritual warfare, I am the same. I want to be among people who are strong in the Lord—those who will fight the good fight, all the time, in Christ.

In Scripture, Demas was a person named for his desertion of Paul. His love for this world ruined him from his supportive role in ministry: *for Demas has forsaken me, having loved this present world, and has departed for Thessalonica . . .* (2 Timothy 4:10). He may have begun well, but the world, as an enemy, had pulled him away.

A young man, John Mark, joined Paul on a missionary journey. For untold reasons, Mark turned back. When the next missionary opportunity came, Paul did not want to have him come along. But Barnabas wanted to take his young cousin (Colossians 4:10).

In the end it was the cause of a sharp division between Paul and Barnabas:

Now Barnabas was determined to take with them John called Mark: But Paul insisted that they should not take with them the one who had departed from them in Pamphylia, and had not gone with them to the work. Then the contention became so sharp that they parted from one another. And so Barnabas took Mark and sailed to Cyprus; but Paul chose Silas and departed, being commended by the brethren to the grace of God.

ACTS 15:37-40

John Mark failed in ministry; yet later on, the Apostle Paul gave him another opportunity to serve. He favorably asked for John Mark when he was imprisoned, as he found him useful: *. . . Get Mark and bring him with you, for he is useful to me for ministry* (2 Timothy 4:11).

Satan Tempts Ananias and Sapphira

Luke wrote about a married couple, two new converts, Ananias and Sapphira, who became casualties in the early church. In the New Testament, in Acts 5, there was a great move of the Holy Spirit, and many were giving their lives to the Lord. As people saw what God was doing, they began selling their possessions and giving them to the church for the work of the ministry.

Ananias and Sapphira also decided to give to the work of the Lord: *But a certain man named Ananias, with Sapphira his wife, sold a possession. And he kept back part of the proceeds, his wife also being aware of it, and brought a certain part and laid it at the apostles' feet* (Acts 5:1-2).

They sold their possessions, gave some of the money to the church and kept back part of it—which was not a sin. However, they did sin when they lied about how much they made and how much they gave to the Lord. The money was theirs to keep or give away. They could have told Peter they were only giving part of the money and told the truth, but because of their greed and pride, they lied. There was no reason to lie, but they wanted to look generous before men.

Satan saw the weakness of their flesh and used it against them. Instead of honestly giving to the Lord, they allowed Satan to interfere with God's work. By walking in their flesh together, they both decided to lie to the Holy Spirit. In Acts 5:3, Peter first confronted Ananias: *But Peter said, "Ananias, why has Satan filled your heart to lie to the Holy Spirit and keep back part of the price of the land for yourself?"*

Notice, God gave Peter a *word of knowledge* (1 Corinthians 12:8). Peter was walking in the Spirit, so he was in tune with the Holy Spirit. He told Ananias: *"While it remained, was it not your own? And after it was sold, was it not in your own control? Why have you conceived this thing in your heart? You have not lied to men but to God."* (Acts 5:4).

This verse is key to this story, because it reveals the real problem—our hearts are desperately wicked (Jeremiah 17:9). Ananias and Sapphira lied to the Holy Spirit; therefore, they had lied to God. God knew Ananias was lying, and the swift penalty was death:

> *Then Ananias, hearing these words, fell down and breathed his last. So great fear came upon all those who heard these things. And the young men arose and wrapped him up, carried him out, and buried him.*
>
> ACTS 5:5-6

Ananias chose to lie to the Lord, and his wife chose to do the same thing:

> *Now it was about three hours later when his wife came in, not knowing what had happened. And Peter answered her, "Tell me whether you sold the land for so much?" She said, "Yes, for so much." Then Peter said to her, "How is it that you have agreed together to test the Spirit of the Lord? Look, the feet of those who have buried your husband are at the door, and they will carry you out."*
>
> ACTS 5:7-9

Sapphira, just like her husband, was killed immediately.

Here are two examples of people who became casualties because they served their flesh and yielded to Satan. When we look at Ananias and Sapphira, we must understand their sin caused the end of their lives.

Uriah the Hittite

In 2 Samuel 11, King David, while taking a break from battle, walked along the roof of his house in Jerusalem. He noticed a beautiful woman bathing. Instead of guarding his heart from the temptations of his flesh, the king lusted after her. Impulsively, he sent for her and then lay with her—he committed adultery, punishable by stoning.

David knew whose wife she belonged to, Uriah, but that never stopped him. Uriah, the husband of Bathsheba, was a faithful and honorable man, a mighty man of valor in King David's army. After David committed adultery, he thought that was the end. But a note arrived from Bathsheba to tell the king something, "David, I am pregnant." You would think David would repent! But no, he continued to plan, and Satan placed different ways for David to hide his sin. When all these schemes failed to cover his sin, he did the unthinkable and had Uriah deliver his own death warrant to Joab, the chief commander of King David's army. Joab would place Uriah in the front of the battle and allow him to be killed by the enemy—can you believe that?

David was a man after God's own heart, but what happened to him? He was now willing to commit murder to cover his sin of adultery. He heard back from Joab—mission accomplished. Uriah is dead. David thought, *Alright!* He took Bathsheba to be his wife, and did not give the matter anymore thought.

What is sad, is that Uriah, even though faithful and loyal to David, became a casualty. David had destroyed one of his own mighty men of valor by causing his death. It was not until a year later, when David was confronted by Nathan the prophet concerning his sin, that he sincerely repented. Tragically, there would be other casualties because of David's carnal choice to sin.

David's own family would bear the impact of his sins. There began certain events that took his family on a destructive domino effect—a downward spiral. They were to experience devastating consequences. David and Bathsheba's newborn son would die. His daughter, Tamar would be raped by her half-brother Amnon. In return, Absalom, angered by his sister's rape, would then kill his half-brother. Absalom would become a rebel in the kingdom and attempt to usurp his father's throne. Outrageously, in the sight of all Israel, he would rape ten of his father's concubines—wives.

David became a casualty of his own sin, but when he fully repented, he regained fellowship with his God, and the joy of his salvation returned (Psalm 51). God, in His goodness and mercy kept David on the throne. Despite his failings, in the future, God was faithful to keep all His promises to David. The Messiah, Jesus Christ, would come from his royal lineage and establish his throne forever (2 Samuel 7:16; Isaiah 9:7).

It is important to remember, our carnal sins never affect just us; they hurt others—our family and friends. When we sin, we harm our own, and they can become casualties. We need to realize and think about who will become a casualty as a direct result of our sin. Hopefully, that knowledge would act as a deterrent and help us resist Satan, as we yield to obey God's Word fully and completely.

THE CHURCH AND THEIR WOUNDED

In our platoon, when the guys went out to fight the enemy, we made a covenant—a code of honor as soldiers—a motto. We vowed to never leave our dead and wounded behind. We carried our wounded and took our injured and dead with us.

On one occasion, our friend Stutes triggered a bouncing-betty—a landmine—an underground explosive. He just lay there with all his limbs blown off—we watched him bleed to death in Pete "Chick" Cicatelli's arms. When we lost Stutes, we picked him up and took him with us—he was just half a body. Can you believe that? But that is exactly what we did; we kept our vow because we loved each other enough.

Tragic scenes like these scar the minds of many brave soldiers. Men who have been in war suffer from PTSD—a serious mental and emotional condition that causes disorders such as nightmares and life-like flashbacks. In the VA, it breaks my heart to see these guys.

I myself have had to spend time in at the Oakland Naval hospital in California being treated for emotional trauma, because of the things I experienced in war; what happened in battle affected my mind tremendously. The mind is strong and carries scars from warfare. Especially as you get older, the memories stay back there forever. I can still see people's wounded faces—it's sad.

Now, at this time in my life, I have developed these episodes where I get a sensation from my navel to my brain. It causes seizures, and, for a time I am not able to speak.

One day, on the way home, after a Wednesday night service, I got to my house. I pulled into my driveway and turned off the engine. All of a sudden, a sensation went from my navel to my throat and then to my brain. It was like gas released into my brain, and in my mind, all of a sudden, I was back in Vietnam. I could see, smell and hear the war in Vietnam. I was being chased by the VC. I got out of my car and started running down the street—hearing gunfire—thinking, "Who is trying to kill me?"

In paranoia, locking the doors and windows, I called my wife. I told her, "Get home quickly!" She found me on the office floor, weeping and crying. I did not feel normal any more. I could not get up in the morning, so I could not teach for four weeks.

War, psychologically, can leave you damaged for the rest of your life. Yet, what does the church do to its wounded? We kick our wounded when they are down, and we leave them behind. It is important to remember that the Church is a hospital. Jesus came for the wounded; He is the Great Physician. Jesus Himself said, "*Those who are well have no need of a physician, but those who are sick. I did not come to call the righteous, but sinners, to repentance*" (Mark 2:17).

Jesus is the greatest example for us to learn how to minister to those who have fallen because of their sin. Remember the way our Lord lovingly ministered to Peter when he had failed. Peter had been sifted—wounded by Satan—but Christ restored him in gentleness. When we are wounded, Christ carries us; He comes through when we need His help the most.

So what should our attitude be towards those who have fallen? The Apostle Paul in Galatians 6:1 explains how to treat and react to those who have been caught up in any sin: *Brethren, if a man is overtaken in any trespass, you who are spiritual restore such a one in a spirit of gentleness, considering yourself lest you also be tempted.* That is real love for your brothers and sisters.

Romans 15:1 (ESV) tells us: *We who are strong have an obligation to bear with the failings of the weak, and not to please ourselves.* It is our Christian duty to reach out to the hurting and help restore them.

The Good Samaritan

The Good Samaritan is an incredible parable that Jesus taught to help a self-righteous lawyer understand, not only how to love your neighbor as yourself, but how to put what Jesus taught into good practice (Luke 10:25-29). It is an important lesson for us to comprehend. This parable will further challenge us, as Christians, to have compassion and mercy toward others in need of our help. Seriously, how do we treat those who have been wounded, regardless of who that person might be? Jesus taught the parable in Luke 10:30-36:

A certain man went down from Jerusalem to Jericho, and fell among thieves, who stripped him of his clothing, wounded him, and departed, leaving him half dead. Now by chance a certain priest came down that road. And when he saw him, he passed by on the other side. Likewise a Levite, when he arrived at the place, came and looked, and passed by on the other side. But a certain Samaritan, as he journeyed, came where he was. And when he saw him, he had compassion. So he went to him and bandaged his wounds, pouring on oil and wine; and he set him on his own animal, brought him to an inn, and took care of him. On the next day, when he departed, he took out two denarii, gave them to the innkeeper, and said to him, 'Take care of him; and whatever more you spend, when I come again, I will repay you.' So which of these three do you think was neighbor to him who fell among the thieves?

Notice how the conversation ended in Luke 10:37. The lawyer answered Jesus' probing question: *And he said, "He who showed mercy on him." Then Jesus said to him, "Go and do likewise."*

We need to get the point of what Jesus is teaching through this parable. So whether there is someone around you who has failed, fallen and repented, or there is a person suffering as a casualty because of another person's sin or their evil acts of violence, we must do all we can to help restore them. Remember, it is not good for Christians to just read the Bible and gain head knowledge, but we must put all these Christian principles into practice—otherwise what good is our Christianity?

Chapter 4

THE WEAPONS OF OUR WARFARE

*For though we walk in the flesh, we do not war
according to the flesh. For the weapons of our
warfare are not carnal but mighty in God for
pulling down strongholds, casting down arguments
and every high thing that exalts itself against the
knowledge of God, bringing every thought into
captivity to the obedience of Christ...*
2 CORINTHIANS 10:3-5

Before we were sent to fight in the Vietnam War, the Marine Corps taught us to master all kinds of weaponry. We were also trained in hand-to-hand combat. There would be times when we would meet the enemy face to face. Our instructors posed to us this important question, "How are you going to defend yourself?" In boot camp they taught us to change our thinking from our civilian mentality, to a soldier's mentality—kill or be killed, plain and simple. In PT

I excelled, and from out of the 500 men, incredibly I was able to finish top of the class, number one in my platoon. I received a Physical Fitness Training Certificate and achieved private first class—which is hard to do.

In training, all the new recruits were given lessons about our armor. Everything they provided for us had a purpose; tactical armor was designed to protect us when we faced the enemy. Instructors showed us how the different pieces of equipment would, not only help guard us, but save our lives.

However, once we arrived, many soldiers did not want to wear some parts of our armor because of the tropical, monsoon climate in Vietnam. The country's dense jungle, constantly saturated by torrential rains, created a heavy atmosphere that was hot and uncomfortably humid. In fact you could smell the humidity, it was disgusting. There was absolutely no relief from the hot humidity and many Marines decided not to wear some of their armor.

New, unseasoned recruits often failed to understand how important every piece of the equipment was to our safety. But they would soon find out that without every piece in place, they became extremely vulnerable to the enemy. As a disciplined Marine, I made sure I had all my body armor in place each day. This armor would help save my life. I took our instructor's training seriously.

THE APOSTLE PAUL'S EXHORTATION

Paul is a person I love—he was a man on the frontlines. As an experienced soldier of Christ, he had skillfully engaged the enemy. He knew he needed the armor of God to protect and defend himself against spiritual attack. Paul was steadfast. He used offensive and defensive weaponry in his spiritual battles. He lived victoriously. During his missionary journeys, he advanced the Gospel message, starting churches throughout many regions of the world.

In the final chapter of the Book of Ephesians, Paul, who wrote this letter while imprisoned, saw the need to give a final exhortation to the believers regarding spiritual warfare. Paul, as a prisoner, had many years, days and hours to study a Roman soldier's armor. He understood their garments were designed to protect them when in any physical battle or engaging their enemies in hand-to-hand combat. Through his close observation, he was able to make great comparisons between the armor of the Roman soldiers, who were guarding him day and night, and God's armor to equip Christians for warfare.

THE ARMOR OF GOD

God, through the power of the Holy Spirit, inspired Paul to write to Christians about the full armor of God, using the spiritual insights he had gained while observing the Roman soldiers guarding him. Paul begins his exhortation in Ephesians 6:10-11: *Finally, my brethren, be strong in the Lord and in the power of His might. Put on the whole armor of God, that you may be able to stand against the wiles of the devil.*

Notice, Paul teaches us that God has given us provision—the full armor of God. He has given us the armor to combat the enemy, and He has also given us the training to engage the enemy. The Lord does not send us into battle defenseless; He has given us protection—the right equipment to become victorious. He instructs us as to where our great strength comes from—the Lord. We cannot go into battle in our own strength. We must depend on the power and might of God.

I think Paul had to make sure we first understood that God is on our side—with His power available to us to fight the battle—before he could tell us about who the enemy is. Christians need to be secure in the Lord before they attempt to take on Satan and his demons. Once we know God is fighting alongside of us, and from where we get our strength, we should remain alert, prepared and ready at all times, knowing who we are fighting against.

While we depend on the strength of the Lord, Paul told us to stand, to face the enemy in battle. He did not tell us to sit, or lie down or give the enemy our backs. We must never just kick back and relax, or the enemy will sneak up and catch us while we are not looking. Remember, Satan is going to come against you at every turn when you are trying to walk with the Lord and serve Him. A Christian must never run from the enemy; we must be strong in the strength of the Lord, stand tall, move forward and never retreat.

In Ephesians 6:12, Paul explains to us who the enemy is and the spiritual warfare we have entered into:

For we do not wrestle against flesh and blood, but against principalities, against powers, against the rulers of the darkness of this age, against spiritual hosts of wickedness in the heavenly places.

Be aware, our foe is spiritual, angelic and wicked. This spiritual battle is very real. Satan has an enormous army; principalities, powers and spiritual hosts are very powerful, but not as powerful as God. Yet, we cannot be foolish and prideful. If we face them without God, in our own strength, we will be defeated by the enemy.

Therefore, Paul, fully knowing who the enemy is, repeats his warning to every believer to put on the whole armor of God in Ephesians 6:13: *Therefore take up the whole armor of God, that you may be able to withstand in the evil day, and having done all, to stand.* This is how we can protect ourselves against Satan, his schemes, and his methods.

Paul knew that not a single piece of armor should ever be missing when engaging the enemy. He desired to give believers facing spiritual combat the ability to, not only protect themselves, but to victoriously overcome their enemy. If they were to accomplish victory on this spiritual battlefield and withstand evil days—hurtful and perilous times, towards those in the Christian faith, they would need a complete understanding of each defensive and offensive piece of armor available to them.

Paul began his instruction to us by explaining each individual piece of the armor we would need. God has pieces of armor for this spiritual warfare to cover us from the top of our head to the bottom of our feet. Each piece is important to protect every part of us, so we have to know what each piece is, what each piece does and how to use each part. Without every piece of armor, we will leave ourselves exposed to the enemy and be in grave danger, so pay close attention and learn from Paul. Remember, he was a man who was in the trenches and experienced spiritual warfare intimately.

Defensive Weapons

The Belt of Truth

In the beginning of Ephesians 6:14, Paul gives us the first piece of the armor: *Stand therefore, having girded your waist with truth.* What does it mean to be girded with truth? The girdle was the Roman soldier's belt. It was not a belt like we have today. The Roman belt was used to support the back and the abdomen, as it wrapped around the waist and gathered up the soldier's garment, to keep it in place so it did not get in the way when he fought. It was also used to hold his sword for battle, along with his dagger for hand-to-hand combat.

Just as the belt was the foundation of the Roman soldier's armor, God's truth is the foundation of our walk with Him. Before we go into spiritual battles, we need to study God's Word and build a foundation of truth. We must hold fast to His truth and gain an understanding of what His truth is. Then we can stand in His truth. Without our faith and trust in God's truth, all the other pieces of armor will be of little use. Without God's truth, the enemy will cause doubt in our minds and we will falter in the battle.

As we study God's Word, we see truth as an attribute in the Trinity of God. God's character is truth. He cannot break His Word, and He always keeps His promises. The Scriptures reveal to us in Numbers 23:19: "*God is not a man, that He should lie, nor a son of man, that He should repent. Has He said, and will He not do? Or has He spoken, and will He not make it good?*"

Then in Titus 1:1-2, Paul expounds on truth as an attribute of God that can be fully trusted:

Paul, a bondservant of God and an apostle of Jesus Christ, according to the faith of God's elect and the acknowledgment of the truth which is according to godliness, in hope of eternal life which God, who cannot lie, promised before time began . . .

Jesus Christ is truth. The Lord told His disciple Thomas: *"I am the way, the truth, and the life. No one comes to the Father except through Me"* (John 14:6). Jesus did not want Thomas to have any doubt planted in his mind from the enemy.

The Holy Spirit is also described as truth: *the Spirit of truth, whom the world cannot receive, because it neither sees Him nor knows Him; but you know Him, for He dwells with you and will be in you* (John 14:17).

God's truth is found in His Word, both in the Law, written in the Old Testament and the Gospel of grace penned in the New Testament: *The entirety of Your word is truth, and every one of Your righteous judgments endures forever* (Psalm 119:160).

In Galatians 2:5, 14, Paul had to rebuke Peter from straying away from the Gospel of grace back into the legality of the Jewish laws:

> *. . . to whom we did not yield submission even for an hour, that the truth of the gospel might continue with you. But when I saw that they were not straightforward about the truth of the gospel, I said to Peter before them all, "If you, being a Jew, live in the manner of Gentiles and not as the Jews, why do you compel Gentiles to live as Jews?"*

The truth of God and His Word is the foundation our faith rests on. Without it, we are not equipped to enter into the spiritual war that is sure to come when we make the decision to walk with Jesus Christ.

The Breastplate of Righteousness

Once the soldier has secured his garments with his belt, he is ready to start putting on the armor. For Christians, the second part of our armor, the breastplate of righteousness follows the belt of truth: *. . . having put on the breastplate of righteousness* (Ephesians 6:14). While the belt supports the back and abdomen, the breastplate protects the front upper body and all the vital organs from the enemy's attacks. In the same way, the righteousness of God protects us in our vulnerability. Remember, Isaiah 64:6 tells us our righteousness is as dirty rags before the Lord: *But we are all like an unclean thing, and all our righteousness are like filthy rags.*

We need the righteousness Christ provided for us when He went to the cross: *and be found in Him* [Christ], *not having my own righteousness, which is from the law, but that which is through faith in Christ, the righteousness which is from God by faith* (Philippians 3:9). His righteousness is our breastplate that covers our vital organs. Our own righteousness would be of little use against the enemy.

Notice, the breastplate covers the front, because we are never to retreat from the enemy or turn our backs on danger. We are to always move forward, trusting by faith the power and might of the Lord, who goes before us in the battles.

Shoes of the Gospel of Peace

The Roman soldier wore sandals with iron nails protruding underneath. They were just long enough to go into the ground to give them greater traction in battle. Remember, the soldiers in Paul's time did not shoot each other from far away. They fought face to face with swords and knives, so the shoes helped them to stay on their feet when they were fighting someone in hand-to-hand combat. They had a solid grip on the ground, so the enemy could not push them down and kill them.

When we go to war, we have to be prepared in advance. We have to be able to stay on our feet. We cannot slip and fall, or worry about stepping on something, so this piece of the armor is to give you a firm foundation to stand on. That is the reason Paul told the Christian: *and having shod your feet with the preparation of the gospel of peace* (Ephesians 6:15). But what does it mean to shod our feet with the Gospel of peace?

As a theologian, Paul, in simple terms told the Church in Rome: *Therefore, having been justified by faith, we have peace with God through our Lord Jesus Christ* (Romans 5:1). Peace only comes through the Gospel of Jesus Christ. If we withstand the attacks of the enemy, then we need to understand, peace with God only comes through Jesus Christ, because we are justified by His sacrifice on the cross.

There is no peace outside of God. We can only have peace with God as we come to know Him intimately. Peace with God eliminates fear. As Christians we must be at peace with God and with each other.

We need to stand with our feet shod with the Gospel of peace in the grace of Jesus Christ. Whenever the door is open, we shall be prepared to share the Gospel of peace with a lost and dying world. The Prophet Isaiah wrote in Isaiah 52:7:

How beautiful upon the mountains are the feet of him who brings good news, who proclaims peace, who brings glad tidings of good things, who proclaims salvation, who says to Zion, "Your God reigns!"

Paul, knowing the Scriptures, quoted Isaiah in Romans 10:15: *And how shall they preach unless they are sent? As it is written: "How beautiful are the feet of those who preach the gospel of peace, who bring glad tidings of good things!"*

The Shield of Faith

Now that we have a strong foothold, standing in the shoes of the Gospel of peace, we have to have the shield of faith to protect us from the enemy's darts. Ephesians 6:16 gives us the next piece of God's armor: *above all, taking the shield of faith with which you will be able to quench all the fiery darts of the wicked one.*

The shield Paul was talking about was made with wood and covered with leather; it was for protection. It was not a small, round shield, but a tall shield. A Roman soldier would be able to stand behind it and withstand the many darts fired from the walls around a city. Roman soldiers could stand side by side, with their shields held together, to protect them from the spears, arrows and fiery darts from the enemy. The shield did not only protect them from the arrows hitting them, but from the fire on their tips. The leather covering the shield was treated, so when the fiery darts hit the shield, the fire would be extinguished.

Our faith in God is the shield we can use to withstand the attacks of the enemy. It not only protects us from the sharp end of the enemies' darts, but it will put out the fire of doubt and confusion, which the enemy wants to spread in our lives. By faith we stand and live in this world, withstanding the lusts of our flesh, the world and Satan. When we have doubts, confusion or condemnation, we have to stay strong in the faith and fight the enemy when he attacks our minds.

Paul said: *For in it* [the Gospel] *the righteousness of God is revealed from faith to faith; as it is written, "The just shall live by faith"* (Romans 1:17). Every day, we live by faith, walk by faith and overcome by faith. First Corinthians 16:13 tells a soldier in Christ: *Watch, stand fast in the faith, be brave, be strong.*

The Helmet of Salvation

Warriors from Roman centurions to our modern Marines and soldiers have worn a helmet to protect their heads. In our spiritual battle, we also have to have something to protect our heads and our minds. Paul said in Ephesians 6:17: *And take the helmet of salvation.* It is a great strategy of Satan to play games with people's minds. Satan loves to attack our minds, and our thoughts, so we have the helmet of salvation to protect us from his attacks.

When we give our lives to Christ, we are saved, and as we abide in Christ, we have no need to worry about our salvation. John 15 explains simply to us the doctrine of abiding in Christ. It is important to understand the only time our salvation is at risk is when we reject Christ and return back to our old lives. Only if we continue to make a practice of sin without repentance, is our salvation at risk (1 Corinthians 6:9-11). The truth is God never leaves us; it is always we who leave Him.

Our salvation is secured by the power of God. It is not by my power or another's power. Consider what Paul said in Romans 1:16: *For I am not ashamed of the gospel of Christ, for it is the power of God to salvation for everyone who believes, for the Jew first and also for the Greek.*

Salvation is obtained through Christ: *And having been perfected, He became the author of eternal salvation to all who obey Him* (Hebrews 5:9). Salvation is for all those who believe and obey Him. Satan has no power over your salvation. He cannot take it away, so put on the helmet of salvation and do not allow Satan to mess with your mind and deceive you.

Offensive Weapons

The Sword of the Spirit

The Roman soldier's greatest weapon was his primary sword, known as the gladius. It was a light, strong, double-edged sword—sharpened on both sides. It was lethal because it could cut from any angle or thrust. A soldier's sword could cleave a man in half with one strike.

Paul tells us in the same verse, Ephesians 6:17, about this important piece of God's armor: . . . *and the sword of the Spirit, which is the Word of God*. The Word of God is the first offensive weapon in our arsenal of weaponry.

All the other pieces of the armor were worn to protect our bodies. The last piece we put on is our weapon—the sword of the Spirit. The sword of the Spirit, which is the Word of God, is the most powerful weapon a Christian has. Paul knew there is power in the Word of God, and without it, we would not have victory. In Hebrews 4:12, Paul described its forcefulness:

For the word of God is living and powerful, and sharper than any two-edged sword, piercing even to the division of soul and spirit, and of joints and marrow, and is a discerner of the thoughts and intents of the heart.

Whenever a church is standing on the Word of God, Satan will try to come in and deceive.

The Word of God

If you are not reading your Bible daily and systematically, you are not going to know anything about the battles you are going to face, and you will be in them without a weapon. Paul the Apostle knew the power of the Word and the importance of studying it. He exhorts us: *Be diligent to present yourself approved to God, a worker who does not need to be ashamed, rightly dividing the word of truth* (2 Timothy 2:15). If you are not growing in your knowledge about God and establishing a relationship with Him, you will never know the power and might He has available for you when you face the enemy.

Everything we read in our Bibles, from the Old Testament to the New Testament, has been written for our example. When we read the Book of Genesis, we learn about creation, God's sovereignty and His power. When we get to the Book of Exodus, we learn about worship. In the Book of Leviticus, we learn about the Law and the holiness of God. As we go through every book in the Bible, there are things we need to learn. Every book of the Bible teaches us something about God. Every book points us to the coming Messiah.

Abraham, Isaac, Jacob, and all the people in the Bible and the things they faced in their lives are written for our example, because we face the same trials, tribulations and challenges today. We can learn from their experiences how they overcame and how they were defeated. If we are not in the Word of God, we really do not have an offensive weapon to use against the enemy.

God's Word is powerful. We need God's Word when the enemy comes against us. It is our only defense. Jesus told us the Holy Spirit will bring God's Word to our remembrance when we need it. In order for Him to bring it to our remembrance, His Word has to be in our heart. When we are spiritually prepared for the battle, we do not depend on ourselves, but on the Lord. When we face the enemy, God will give us the words we should speak. He will enable and empower us for the battle.

We have to read God's Word and study it, so the Holy Spirit can give us the right things to say when we are in the battle: *"But the Helper, the Holy Spirit, whom the Father will send in My name, He will teach you all things, and bring to your remembrance all things that I said to you"* (John 14:26).

This is what the Holy Spirit will do for us when we are faced with the enemy, but if we do not know God's Word, He cannot bring it to our remembrance because nothing is there. You must read and study His Word so you can use it effectively as a sword in the battles of life.

Jesus Used the Sword

When we are faced with the enemy, our greatest weapon is God's Word. A soldier's sword can be used against himself if he does not know how to use it. In the same way, if we are not trained in the Word, the enemy can use God's Word against us. That is what Satan tried to do when he confronted Jesus in the wilderness.

In Matthew 4:1-10, we have Jesus' encounter with Satan: *Then Jesus was led up by the Spirit into the wilderness to be tempted by the devil* (Matthew 4:1).

Jesus prepared for His battle with Satan by denying His flesh: *And when He had fasted forty days and forty nights, afterward He was hungry* (Matthew 4:2). He did not eat or drink anything for 40 days.

Miraculously, Jesus, Moses and Elijah were able to fast for 40 days and 40 nights without dying. You may ask, "How long can a person survive without food?" Alan D. Lieberson, a medical doctor and lawyer, noted in *Scientific American*, on November 8, 2004, that if you fast for five days you experience hunger pains and after 10 to14 days you starve to death.

Satan thought he picked the perfect time to tempt Jesus. He supposed Jesus was too weak to fight: *Now when the tempter came to Him, he said, "If You are the Son of God, command that these stones become bread"* (Matthew 4:3). The temptation came after Jesus was led by the Holy Spirit into the wilderness and had fasted 40 days and nights. He denied himself food, and the moment Satan saw Jesus was hungry, he tempted him physically. Jesus could have taken rocks and made bread, but He denied His human nature. The thing to remember is not how long Jesus fasted, but that He denied His hunger for food.

Satan waits until you are physically, emotionally and spiritually weak to come and tempt you. If you are not in the Word of God and you are not in prayer, Satan will defeat you. He will wipe you out. That is why so many people backslide. They are not walking with God, being led by the Holy Spirit. They have no offensive weapon against Satan. This is why young Christians do not really understand or have the power to overcome when temptation comes. They are not in the Word of God—they have no weapon against Satan. They are not able to fight the enemy.

Christians get defeated by thoughts, doubts and temptations. Jesus resisted Satan with the Word of God. He used the sword of the Spirit to combat Satan's temptation: *But He answered and said, "It is written, 'Man shall not live by bread alone, but by every word that proceeds from the mouth of God' "* (Matthew 4:4). Jesus was quoting Deuteronomy 8:3. He told Satan that man survives off of spiritual food, not physical food. We need to be in the Word of God. The Word of God sustains us.

When Satan could not get Jesus to give into physical temptation, he tried to get Him emotionally:

> *Then the devil took Him up into the holy city, set Him on the pinnacle of the temple, and said to Him, "If You are the Son of God, throw Yourself down. For it is written: 'He shall give His angels charge over you,' and, 'In their hands they shall bear you up, lest you dash your foot against a stone.' "*
>
> MATTHEW 4:5-6

Satan is smart. He used the Word of God, but he misquoted it. It is important to understand, Satan will use Scripture, too; if you do not know the Word of God, you will not know he is twisting it to suit his purposes, as he did in this Scripture (Psalm 91). This is how people are deceived by false religions. False teachers use the Scriptures, and those people, who do not know the Word of God, are easily led astray.

Many cults use the Scriptures but they misquote them or they only use a small portion, out of context, to make it sound right. They get that from Satan. He always tries to imitate the Lord, as he transforms himself into an angel of light (2 Corinthians 11:14).

Jesus again used the sword of the Spirit to respond to Satan's temptation. Jesus quoted Deuteronomy 6:16 in His response in Matthew 4:7: *Jesus said to him, "It is written again, 'You shall not tempt the Lord your God.' "*

We do not know every trial or temptation a person experiences, but Jesus has made it very clear—there is always a way of escape. While Satan makes it seem as if there is no escaping sin, Jesus always provides a way out.

When Satan could not tempt him physically or emotionally, he tried to tempt him spiritually, in Matthew 4:8-9:

> *Again, the devil took Him up on an exceedingly high mountain, and showed Him all the kingdoms of the world and their glory. And he said to Him, "All these things I will give You if You will fall down and worship me."*

As before, Jesus came back with the Word of God: *Then Jesus said to him, "Away with you, Satan! For it is written, 'You shall worship the Lord your God, and Him only you shall serve' "* (Matthew 4:10).

Again, Jesus quoted from the Pentateuch, Deuteronomy 6:13. We are not to serve any other gods, but the One, True, Living God—Jehovah.

Can you imagine how many rich and famous people today have bowed their knees to Satan? They have fallen for the temptation of fame and glory in exchange for their soul. Just for money and success and time in the limelight. None of those things will last; they are all temporal.

Once Jesus withstood these three temptations, Satan left: *Then the devil left Him, and behold, angels came and ministered to Him* (Matthew 4:11). The angels came to minister to Jesus and prepared Him something to eat.

In Luke 4:13, it says: *Now when the devil had ended every temptation, he departed from Him until an opportune time.* Notice, Satan only left Jesus for a season, waiting to come back another time with other powerful temptations. Satan never leaves us alone; he will even be at your deathbed trying to discourage and depress you. That is why, as believers, we need to know the Scriptures and be there for those who are dying. Do not allow any of those who are dying to have their minds idle because idle minds are Satan's playground. Satan never gives up; he will never stop until he is cast into the Lake of Fire.

Jesus is the Word

When we think about the power of God's Word, we have to remember, *In the beginning was the Word, and the Word was with God, and the Word was God. He was in the beginning with God* (John 1:1-2). The power of the Word is the power of God, and it is unlimited and without match. There is no enemy more powerful than God and His Word.

That is the power we have available to us. When we know God and we know His Word, we do not have to fear the enemy, because the Word of God will defeat him:

> *I have written to you, fathers, because you have known Him who is from the beginning. I have written to you, young men, because you are strong, and the word of God abides in you, and you have overcome the wicked one.*
> 1 JOHN 2:14

In the beginning, it was by the power of God's spoken Word that the universe was formed: *By faith we understand that the worlds were framed by the word of God, so that the things which are seen were not made of things which are visible* (Hebrews 11:3). Think about the power it took to create the universe from nothing. It is incredible.

> *All things were made through Him* [the Word], *and without Him nothing was made that was made. And the Word became flesh and dwelt among us, and we beheld His glory, the glory as of the only begotten of the Father, full of grace and truth.*
> JOHN 1:3, 14

God's Word became flesh, and Jesus walked among men and man beheld the glory of God's Son—His Only Begotten Son.

As the Word of God was there at the beginning of all time, He [Christ] will be there at the end: *He was clothed with a robe dipped in blood, and His name is called The Word of God* (Revelation 19:13). As we grow in our knowledge of God's Word, the greatest comfort we can have is to know He is with us, and we have His Word available to us at any time. It is not only a sword to defend ourselves from the enemy, but it gives great strength and comfort as we go through the trials and tribulations of this life.

Prayer

God has given us the perfect weapons to combat the enemy, and He will be with us in the battle. We have the ability to put on the full armor of God and resist the devil. Once we put on the full armor of the Lord, there is one more exhortation from Paul:

> . . . *praying always with all prayer and supplication in the Spirit, being watchful to this end with all perseverance and supplication for all the saints—and for me, that utterance may be given to me, that I may open my mouth boldly to make known the mystery of the gospel, for which I am an ambassador in chains; that in it I may speak boldly, as I ought to speak.*
>
> EPHESIANS 6:18-20

God knew the enemies we would face, and He did not leave us unprepared or unable to defend ourselves. He not only gave us His Word, but we have another powerful offensive weapon; we have prayer. Every saint in the Bible understood the power of prayer. From Moses to David, God's people sought the Lord in prayer before going to battle. If you look at the great success the children of Israel had in any battle, it always began in prayer.

Moses recorded God's direction for battle:

"Rise, take your journey, and cross over the River Arnon. Look, I have given into your hand Sihon the Amorite, king of Heshbon, and his land. Begin to possess it, and engage him in battle. This day I will begin to put the dread and fear of you upon the nations under the whole heaven, who shall hear the report of you, and shall tremble and be in anguish because of you. "

DEUTERONOMY 2:24-25

David inquired of the Lord before entering into battle*: Therefore David inquired of the Lord, saying, "Shall I go and attack these Philistines?" And the Lord said to David, "Go and attack the Philistines, and save Keilah"* (1 Samuel 23:2).

Joshua, in communion with the Lord, received these important instructions:

Now the Lord said to Joshua: "Do not be afraid, nor be dismayed; take all the people of war with you, and arise, go up to Ai. See, I have given into your hand the king of Ai, his people, his city, and his land."

JOSHUA 8:1

When these leaders failed to inquire of the Lord, they were defeated. When they inquired of the Lord, He told them exactly how to defeat the enemy. That is how God works. He not only empowers us with His Word, but He will guide and direct us when we come to Him in prayer. He will tell us whether we should enter the battle or not. Like the children of Israel, we have to spend time in prayer with the Lord if we want to have victory in our lives.

If we do not spend time in prayer with the Lord, we will not have victory. If we are not praying, Satan does not have to worry about us, because we have no power against him. Look at what William Cowper, an evangelical Christian in the eighteenth century, wrote: "And Satan trembles when he sees the weakest saint upon his knees."

Satan hates us when we are on our knees because we are coming against him. Prayer gives us power. It does not matter how strong you are, how talented you are or how much wisdom you may have, you cannot defeat the enemy alone; you will fail. We can only win the battles on our knees before God. This is the position of humility and submitting our will before God.

Remember, if you are a Christian, you are in a spiritual war; you do not have a choice. Satan is going to come against you when you give your life to Jesus. Just as he tempted Jesus and tried to make Him deny the will of the Father, he is going to try and make us turn from the Lord. Satan does not want us to complete the work that the Lord has for us in building the Kingdom of God. If we do not spend time with God in prayer, we will fail. We will not have the power to follow the path God has for us.

When Jesus was preparing for the betrayal of Judas and His arrest, He went to the Garden of Gethsemane to spend time in prayer with the Lord. Jesus knew the battle He was going to face. He knew Satan wanted Him to fail. The souls of mankind were in the balance, and Jesus knew He had to be with His Father to face the physical torture that would come: *He went a little farther and fell on His face, and prayed, saying, "O My Father, if it is possible, let this cup pass from Me; nevertheless, not as I will, but as You will"* (Matthew 26:39).

Knowing the great trial and the physical pain He would endure on the cross, Jesus prayed to the Father and accepted His will. During the time He spent alone with His Father, He was empowered to die for the sins of the world and be victorious over death.

Pray Always

When Paul the Apostle was facing death, he prayed for the suffering saints, the Church and for God's will. He was always in prayer: *Therefore we* [Paul, Silvanus and Timothy] *also pray always for you that our God would count you worthy of this calling, and fulfill all the good pleasure of His goodness and the work of faith with power* (2 Thessalonians 1:11).

While Paul was always praying for the body of Christ, he understood the need for the believers to also be in prayer all the time. He had already exhorted them: *Rejoice always, pray without ceasing, in everything give thanks; for this is the will of God in Christ Jesus for you* (1Thessalonians 5:16-18).

The Apostle Paul understood the power of prayer and asked for the Church to pray for him while he was going through great trials: *Now I beg you, brethren, through the Lord Jesus Christ, and through the love of the Spirit, that you strive together with me in prayers to God for me* (Romans 15:30).

Paul knew and understood spiritual warfare, because he lived in it every day. His life was a constant battle, and yet, he had great power because he was always in prayer. He used the words *pray always* and *pray without ceasing*, because he wanted the Church to understand the need to pray on every occasion and in all seasons. There is nothing too little to bring before the Lord. He wants to guide and direct our lives. He wants us to have victory in the battles; therefore, He calls us to pray without ceasing, so He can encourage and strengthen us.

Types of Prayer

Many times, Christians do not understand the things Paul wrote about prayer. They do not understand what it means to always be praying. They see the pastor pray, and they pray before meals and before bed, so they do not know what it means to pray without ceasing. They think you have to close your eyes and fold your hands in order to pray.

It is really easy to pray without ceasing when you realize there are many ways to pray. You do not have to close your eyes or fold your hands. You do not have to kneel or stand a certain way. Prayer is just communication with God. Just like when we talk with our families and friends, we communicate better when we have no distractions. God just wants our hearts and minds to be open and focused on Him.

If I am going to be in prayer all the time, I will pray in many different ways. One of the greatest times I will spend in prayer is in my personal and private prayer time. Jesus instructed His disciples in prayer, in Matthew 6:6: *"But you, when you pray, go into your room, and when you have shut your door, pray to your Father who is in the secret place; and your Father who sees in secret will reward you openly."*

Jesus was teaching them about private prayer. This is done alone, with no one else. That is why He told them to go to a prayer room. You do not have to go to a specific room for your private prayer. But, you do want to go somewhere without your phone, the computer, the television and anything else that will interrupt your quiet time with the Lord. You can pray while you are driving down the freeway with your eyes wide open. You can pray for others in your private prayer time, but you do not have to share anything about your private prayers with others. They are between you and God alone.

Family prayer is just as important as private prayer. I believe one of the things breaking up marriages is the lack of family prayer. Families do not spend time together, and everybody has their own agenda. They are not coming together before the Lord, speaking to God and, more importantly, waiting to hear from Him.

I know we are living in a busy society, but it is good to have times to gather together with your wife and children in prayer. During that time, ask God to surround your family with His angels. Especially pray for your children who are not walking with the Lord. You may have a son or daughter on drugs or alcohol, and they will not listen to you. God will listen to you clearly, and God will do a better job working in the lives of your children.

God is amazing in the way He hears our prayers. There is power in prayer. Satan wants your children, and he wants your marriage. Satan wants you. If you are not spending time in prayer and the Word of God with your family, then you do not have a defense against his schemes.

When Paul was instructing husbands and wives in Ephesians 5, he told husbands: *Husbands, love your wives, just as Christ also loved the church and gave Himself for her, that He might sanctify and cleanse her with the washing of water by the word* (Ephesians 5:25-26).

When Paul told husbands to wash their wives by the water of the Word, he was exhorting them to spend time in God's Word and prayer with their wives. It is the husband's responsibility to ensure the family comes together in prayer and the Word. If he does not do it, wives need to step in and lead their children in communion with the Lord.

Just as you spend time together as a family in prayer, it is also important to pray in groups with others outside your family. Jesus said: *For where two or three are gathered together in My name, I am there in the midst of them* (Matthew 18:20). When there are just two people praying together, Jesus will be there. You do not need a big group, but as you come together, you can pray for one another, pray for the nation and pray for the world. When Christians come together to pray, Jesus is there in their midst and there is great power.

Whether we are praying alone or with others, when we direct our prayers to God, He hears and He responds. When John wrote the Book of Revelation, he revealed where our prayers go: *And the smoke of the incense, with the prayers of the saints, ascended before God from the angel's hand* (Revelation 8:4).

All our prayers ascend to the throne of God, and none are left unanswered. God hears all of them, and they are answered in His time.

God will empower us and enable us to use every piece of the armor of God when we spend time with Him in prayer. All spiritual things must begin and end in prayer. We should never engage the enemy without prayer, and since we never know when he will strike, we need to always be prepared—praying always.

Paul called on the believer to pray so he would have spiritual strength to be able to withstand the enemy. Without spiritual power from the Lord, no Christian can face spiritual warfare. We are no match for Satan. Seriously, you will not defeat the enemy—he will defeat you.

STRENGTH IN GOD'S WEAPONS

From the Old Testament to the New Testament, God's people relied on God and His spiritual armor to withstand the attacks of the enemy. David was a great example of a warrior, both physically and spiritually. In the Psalms, he often wrote of where his strength came from: *I will love You, O Lord, my strength* (Psalm 18:1). Then he wrote in Psalm 27:1: *The Lord is my light and my salvation; whom shall I fear? The Lord is the strength of my life; of whom shall I be afraid?*

David, constantly in battle, attributed his fighting ability to the Lord, who taught him how to fight the battles of life. He declared:

> *Blessed be the Lord my Rock, who trains my* hands for war, *and* my fingers for battle—*my loving kindness and my fortress, my high tower and my deliverer, my shield and the One in whom I take refuge, who subdues my people under me.*
> PSALM 144:1, 2

David was not afraid because he knew God was his protection and refuge. As the sweet Psalmist of Israel, he wrote: *... He is the saving refuge of His anointed* (Psalm 28:8). He knew God personally and wrote what his God had become to him during the battles he faced in life: *The Lord is my rock and my fortress and my deliverer; my God, my strength, in whom I will trust; my shield and the horn of my salvation, my stronghold.* (Psalm 18:2).

Knowing the life of David and the many battles he fought, we can take refuge in the knowledge that God will be our strength and comfort, as we engage in the spiritual warfare set before us. Then, we can speak the same words of David, safe in the knowledge of God's great love, grace and mercy.

The weapons of the Word of God and prayer are our spiritual armor. They are both offensive and defensive weapons. Offensively, we should be studying God's Word every day, so we can grow spiritually and have a closer walk with the Lord. Once you know the Word, you can use it defensively when the enemy twists the Scriptures to trip you up. You will not be deceived like Eve, because you will know he is lying, and you will be able to use the Word to correct him, just as Jesus did in the wilderness.

As we read the Bible in order to grow spiritually and be prepared for the attacks of our enemies, we need to be in prayer—in communion with God—to stay spiritually strong. When the attacks come and we are weak in our faith, we use prayer as our defensive weapon, as we bring our trials before the Lord in prayer. In those times of fellowship with Him, He will comfort and strengthen us.

Both together and individually, the Word of God and prayer are the most important weapons of offense God has provided for us. Without these vital weapons we cannot stand against the enemy.

Knowing we will face spiritual warfare in our walk as Christians, we can be encouraged in the great comfort and strength God provides for us through His Word and prayer. God has provided these necessary weapons for us to use when the enemy attacks us, but we are responsible to train and learn how to use these spiritual weapons. God will show us how to use them when we spend time with Him in His Word and in prayer.

Chapter 5

CHRIST OUR CAPTAIN

And it came to pass, when Joshua was by Jericho, that he lifted his eyes and looked, and behold, a Man stood opposite him with His sword drawn in His hand. And Joshua went to Him and said to Him, "Are You for us or for our adversaries?" So He said, "No, but as Commander of the army of the Lord I have now come."
JOSHUA 5:13-14

CHAIN OF COMMAND

A troubled life in my past caused me to have tremendous anger and rage, and with no self-control whatsoever, I often ended up in fights. On one occasion, I had beaten someone so badly they had to be taken to the hospital. As a result, I landed up in front of a judge. At the court hearing, I had a choice—jail time or enter the military.

I would be transported to the Marine Corps Recruit Depot, a military installation in San Diego, for my initial training, and for more extensive training later, I would be transferred to Camp Pendleton. I had left by bus and arrived in San Diego as an enlisted subordinate with the other new recruits. We quickly learned who was in charge.

One of the first things the drill instructors did was to strip us of our identity. They began to yell, cuss and scream degrading comments at us. Certain individuals were humiliated in front of everyone. Understand, we were referred to as maggots, and scumbags, and we could not even be called a Marine until we passed all the training.

Barbers uniformly gave us all buzzed haircuts. Then we had to take a shower together, while at the same time, submitting to officers who shouted orders at us to do pushups. Imagine seventy men in one shower, close to each other, doing push-ups, going up and down while the drill instructors screamed orders at us.

Once that initiation was completed, we were given our equipment to carry and were made to understand the responsibility for the upkeep. Imagine, we were no longer civilians, comfortable within society; we were in training to become disciplined Marines in a matter of 13 weeks and as such, we now belonged to the U.S. government. Boot camp was a rude awakening for new enlistees.

Understandably, within the military there is a distinct chain of command to follow. By virtue of superior rank, officers exacted authority over us. They were responsible to supervise us and closely examined our personal performances. Officers routinely inspected our weapons to make sure our gear and equipment were operational. They maintained order, discipline, control, security and enforced regulations as deemed necessary.

A Marine is not only trained physically, but his moral character is shaped. In the military, there is a strict code of conduct to be followed. In our training, there are fourteen traits that our instructors instilled in our character: judgment, justice, dependability, integrity, decisiveness, tact, initiative, enthusiasm, bearing, unselfishness, knowledge, loyalty, endurance and courage.

Marines are our nation's "most ready force" and, as such, immediately respond to an officer's direct commands. Every directive—written orders—was followed without excuse or exception. If sent out on a special mission, our goal was to return with our mission accomplished. A Marine's main objective is to save lives and protect government property. A Marine could be called upon at any time to give the ultimate sacrifice—his life. That is the reality of what you sign up for. In the Marines, you agreed to willingly and sacrificially give your life for the freedom and safety of others.

Any Marine who showed disregard for authority was logged and dealt with immediately. Those who disobeyed and did not comply with any orders from an officer could be placed in detention—held in custody—and at worst, be court-martialed and suffer a dishonorable discharge.

Once we were in Vietnam, those in authority gave us commands, but they did so from safe positions. If necessary, those orders would send us right into the middle of the battlefield.

At times, led by those in authority, we were given a master plan. We would get together and look over a map of the territory to strategize how to attack a certain place. A decision would be made whether to call in the airplane to drop mortars or send in our troops. Usually a mission would begin at night, about ten o'clock in the evening. A village would be surrounded, and in the early morning, with an element of surprise, we would catch our enemies coming out of their houses. Sometimes in warfare our troop's maneuver was to do a sweep and destroy everything in sight—the village was burned down. War is never pleasant—the cost for freedom is high.

CHARACTER COUNTS

It is important to understand that every solider of God has to go through training. If you do not go through this training, in the kingdom of God you will never be able to be placed in the front lines. You will be as a soldier unequipped for battle—you will be killed instantly.

God also expects us to submit to the chain of command established in the Church. We need to be submissive and obey those He has placed over us—pastors and elders. The Apostle Paul exhorted Christians in Hebrews 12:13 to:

> *Obey those who rule over you, and be submissive, for they watch out for your souls, as those who must give account. Let them do so with joy and not with grief, for that would be unprofitable for you.*

Chastening also becomes a part of our character training as Christians. When we do not obey the Lord we are chastened by Him. Just as a father loves his son and corrects him, so God corrects us:

> *If you endure chastening, God deals with you as with sons; for what son is there whom a father does not chasten? But if you are without chastening, of which all have become partakers, then you are illegitimate and not sons. Furthermore, we have had human fathers who corrected us, and we paid them respect. Shall we not much more readily be in subjection to the Father of spirits and live? For they indeed for a few days chastened us as seemed best to them, but He for our profit, that we may be partakers of His holiness. Now no chastening seems to be joyful for the present, but painful; nevertheless, afterward it yields the peaceable fruit of righteousness to those who have been trained by it.*
>
> HEBREWS 12:7-11

It is important to understand that holiness is the code of conduct for every Christian. The Bible exhorts us to live by the Lord's high moral standard: *but as He who called you is holy, you also be holy in all your conduct, because it is written, "Be holy, for I am holy"* (1 Peter 1:15-16).

Our Christian conduct identifies us as a soldier of Christ. We belong to the Lord and must be subject to Him in everything. Our behavior should befit our call as a Christian; therefore, contentment, unity, faith, virtue, knowledge, self-control, perseverance, godliness, kindness and love, not only shape our lives, but help us in the battle against our enemies. The Apostle Paul clearly defines what our Christian character should be like:

> *Only let your conduct be worthy of the gospel of Christ, so that whether I come and see you or am absent, I may hear of your affairs, that you stand fast in one spirit, with one mind striving together for the faith of the gospel.*
> PHILIPPIANS 1:27

> *Let your conduct be without covetousness; be content with such things as you have. For He Himself has said, "I will never leave you nor forsake you."*
> HEBREWS 13:5

> *But also for this very reason, giving all diligence, add to your faith virtue, to virtue knowledge, to knowledge self-control, to self-control perseverance, to perseverance godliness, to godliness brotherly kindness, and to brotherly kindness love.*
> 2 PETER 1:5-7

Prayerfully ask the Lord to train you in these areas of your Christian character.

It is essential to be reminded that we need the mentality of a soldier as we go into battle. Paul, in preparing us to face spiritual warfare, did just that when he said: *". . . be strong in the Lord and in the power of His might"* (Ephesians 6:10). Remember, courage is indispensable in battle.

BE STRONG AND COURAGEOUS

Courage and strength were key characteristics that needed to be built in the life of the new, chosen leader of Israel— Joshua. You see, Moses would not lead the people of Israel over the River Jordan and into the Promised Land. Joshua, Moses' servant, was now elevated to the rank of chief leader over Israel. The Lord instructed Moses:

> *"Go up to the top of Pisgah, and lift your eyes toward the west, the north, the south, and the east; behold it with your eyes, for you shall not cross over this Jordan. But command Joshua, and encourage him and strengthen him; for he shall go over before this people, and he shall cause them to inherit the land which you will see."*
> DEUTERONOMY 3:27-28

Joshua was to be encouraged and strengthened by Moses. The word *strengthened* comes from a root word meaning: to be alert, physically (on foot) or mentally (in courage). Other meanings include: confirm, be courageous (of good courage, steadfastly minded), establish, fortify, harden, increase, prevail, strengthen (self), make strong (obstinate, speed).

Joshua needed to be a strong leader, and he had to be undaunted in mind—fearless. God encouraged Joshua and gave him the strategy for success, for all his battles, during his entire lifetime:

After the death of Moses the servant of the Lord, it came to pass that the Lord spoke to Joshua the son of Nun, Moses' assistant, saying: "Moses My servant is dead. Now therefore, arise, go over this Jordan, you and all this people, to the land which I am giving to them—the children of Israel. Every place that the sole of your foot will tread upon I have given you, as I said to Moses. From the wilderness and this Lebanon as far as the great river, the River Euphrates, all the land of the Hittites, and to the Great Sea toward the going down of the sun, shall be your territory. No man shall be able to stand before you all the days of your life; as I was with Moses, so I will be with you. I will not leave you nor forsake you. Be strong and of good courage, for to this people you shall divide as an inheritance the land which I swore to their fathers to give them. Only be strong and very courageous, that you may observe to do according to all the law which Moses My servant commanded you; do not turn from it to the right hand or to the left, that you may prosper wherever you go. This Book of the Law shall not depart from your mouth, but you shall meditate in it day and night, that you may observe to do according to all that is written in it. For then you will make your way prosperous, and then you will have good success. Have I not commanded you? Be strong and of good courage; do not be afraid, nor be dismayed, for the Lord your God is with you wherever you go."

JOSHUA 1:1-9

Notice, repeatedly, God encouraged Joshua to be strong and of good courage. His success in battle was dependent on the use of his spiritual weaponry—his obedience to God's Word; he was to meditate in it day and night. God had given His servant Joshua marching orders—his life-time tour of duty was to take the land of Canaan. His season of leadership was exciting; God had given Israel the land. God's people would no longer wander in the wilderness; Joshua would finally lead the children of Israel into the Promised Land.

Forty years prior, they had been on the borders of this fertile land, full of milk and honey, but ten fearful, weak-hearted leaders negatively influenced a nation. Sadly, because of unbelief, an almost 11-day journey, which had brought them near to the Promise Land, caused them to wander in a great and dreadful wilderness. During this time, the nation was purged of all those who had unbelief in their hearts. Now, once more, they stood on the threshold of the Promised Land—a young nation with a new, young, and fearless leader, Joshua.

Joshua and the children of Israel crossed over the Jordan River, which, spiritually speaking is a symbol of reckoning the old man to be dead. Then, while the waters were still heaped up on two sides, God told the people to go back and take twelve stones, and place them in the midst of the Jordan as a covenant of God's blessing, as the children of Israel went into the Promised Land:

> *And it came to pass, when all the people had completely crossed over the Jordan, that the Lord spoke to Joshua, saying: "Take for yourselves twelve men from the people, one man from every tribe, and command them, saying, 'Take for yourselves twelve stones from here, out of the midst of the Jordan, from the place where the priests' feet stood firm. You shall carry them over with you and leave them in the lodging place where you lodge tonight.'" Then Joshua called the twelve men whom he had appointed from the children of Israel, one man from every tribe; and Joshua said to them: "Cross over before the ark of the Lord your God into the midst of the Jordan, and each one of you take up a stone on his shoulder, according to the number of the tribes of the children of Israel, that this may be a sign among you when your children ask in time to come, saying, 'What do these stones mean to you?' Then you shall answer them that the waters of the Jordan were cut off before the ark of the covenant of the Lord; when it crossed over the Jordan, the waters of the Jordan were cut off. And these stones shall be for a memorial to the children of Israel forever."*
>
> JOSHUA 4:1-7

The children of Israel did as Joshua commanded. Then Joshua, took twelve stones from the midst of the Jordan from the place where the priests stood firm with the ark as a memorial of that day when the waters were cut off before the ark of the covenant of the Lord. He also placed twelve stones, piled high, as a memorial in the Jordan River where the priest stood with ark, as the people crossed over. Therefore, when the waters of the Jordan River lowered, the stones became visible, and the children would ask their fathers, "What are these stones?" Then they would retell the story of God's mighty power; that as He dried up the Red Sea, so He dried up the waters of the Jordan until they had crossed over.

As God had been with Moses, He promised, He would be with Joshua. In His mighty power, God parted the waters of the Jordan and strengthened Joshua, to lead the children of Israel across it and into the Promised Land:

On that day the Lord exalted Joshua in the sight of all Israel; and they feared him, as they had feared Moses, all the days of his life (Joshua 4:14).

Crossing over the Jordan River into the Promised Land was going to be a life of victory for the children of Israel. You see, the land they left behind—Egypt, was a life of slavery and defeat.

THE BATTLE IS THE LORD'S

As Christians, God leads us, as it were, across our *Jordan River*—where we reckon the old man to be dead—dying to self. Like Israel's enemies that feared them as they came into the Promised Land (Joshua 2:9-11), our enemies will now fear us as we come into our *Promised Land*—the life of victory. Why? As we remain obedient to God's Word and meditate in it day and night, as Joshua was instructed, then the Lord will fight for us. Always keep in mind, the battle no longer belongs to us; the battles we face in life are the Lord's.

Listen, when a great multitude came against Israel—an invading army from Moab—Ammon and others closed in about them. King Jehoshaphat set himself to seek the Lord and proclaimed a fast throughout all Judea. They came together to seek the Lord that He might save them (2 Chronicles 20:1-13).

Then the Spirit of the Lord came upon Jahaziel, the son of Zechariah, and he said to the people and the king: . . . *"Thus says the Lord to you: 'Do not be afraid nor dismayed because of this great multitude, for the battle is not yours, but God's'* (2 Chronicles 20:15). Then Jahaziel gave them God's plans for the battle:

> *"Tomorrow go down against them. They will surely come up by the Ascent of Ziz, and you will find them at the end of the brook before the Wilderness of Jeruel. You will not need to fight in this battle. Position yourselves, stand still and see the salvation of the Lord, who is with you, O Judah and Jerusalem!' Do not fear or be dismayed; tomorrow go out against them, for the Lord is with you."*
>
> 2 CHRONICLES 20:16-17

And Jehoshaphat bowed his head with his face to the ground, and all Judah and the inhabitants of Jerusalem bowed before the Lord, worshiping the Lord. Then the Levites of the children of the Kohathites and of the children of the Korahites stood up to praise the Lord God of Israel with voices loud and high.

2 CHRONICLES 20:18-19

So they rose early in the morning and went out into the Wilderness of Tekoa; and as they went out, Jehoshaphat stood and said, "Hear me, O Judah and you inhabitants of Jerusalem: Believe in the Lord your God, and you shall be established; believe His prophets, and you shall prosper." And when he had consulted with the people, he appointed those who should sing to the Lord, and who should praise the beauty of holiness, as they went out before the army and were saying:

*"Praise the Lord,
For His mercy endures forever."*

Now when they began to sing and to praise, the Lord set ambushes against the people of Ammon, Moab, and Mount Seir, who had come against Judah; and they were defeated. For the people of Ammon and Moab stood up against the inhabitants of Mount Seir to utterly kill and destroy them. And when they had made an end of the inhabitants of Seir, they helped to destroy one another.

2 CHRONICLES 20:20-23

Judah was comforted by the Lord's presence; they did not need to be afraid. God gave them their strategy against their enemies—commit the battle to the Lord. They remained still, waiting on the Lord for His deliverance. While the people praised the Lord and believed what He had promised them, He gave them the victory.

As the people gave themselves over to worship, the Lord set ambushes against their enemies and they were defeated! What was the result of trusting the Lord in the battle?

> *So when Judah came to a place overlooking the wilderness, they looked toward the multitude; and there were their dead bodies, fallen on the earth. No one had escaped . . . Then they returned, every man of Judah and Jerusalem, with Jehoshaphat in front of them, to go back to Jerusalem with joy, for the Lord had made them rejoice over their enemies. So they came to Jerusalem, with stringed instruments and harps and trumpets, to the house of the Lord. And the fear of God was on all the kingdoms of those countries when they heard that the Lord had fought against the enemies of Israel. Then the realm of Jehoshaphat was quiet, for his God gave him rest all around.*
>
> 2 CHRONICLES 20:24-30

Notice how God struck fear in the hearts of their enemies; they knew the Lord was fighting on behalf of Judah. We can learn so much about spiritual warfare from what is written in God's Word. If you are living a life of defeat, examine how you are fighting your battles. Many times, we are trying to fight the battles ourselves, and we conflict with the Lord's strategy against the enemy. Why not put into practice some of the strategies we have learned from 2 Chronicles 20:1-30, and exchange defeat for victory?

Many times, we think God's strategies are not going to work; we think our plans are going to be better. So, we are constantly being defeated, because we do not allow God to fight for us.

God is on the throne, but I say this: "We need to learn to take instructions and learn to submit to the Lordship of Jesus Christ." There is no way we are ever going to experience victory over our enemy's camp unless we submit to Christ. If we do not do this, then the enemy will constantly hassle and defeat us.

Examine your life, and honestly assess whether you are fully submitted to the Lordship of Jesus Christ. What did you find? Are you a self-centered person? Have you placed your will secondary, so that you can do what God tells you to do? Submission will often hurt as you die to self, when you have to obediently do something that you do not want to do. But know one thing; God will give you the strength, power and victory as you do those things He has called you to do. He will bless you so much—tremendously.

COMMANDER OF THE ARMY OF THE LORD

God would fight for Israel, but Joshua, before the battle, would encounter the Commander of the Army of the LORD. Joshua observed a person up on a hill, looking over Jericho, with a sword drawn.

As Joshua took a closer look, suddenly he fell to his knees as he recognized that the Commander was a theophany—Jesus Christ visible in the Old Testament. Joshua was astonished, and his attitude completely changed:

> *And it came to pass, when Joshua was by Jericho, that he lifted his eyes and looked, and behold, a Man stood opposite him with His sword drawn in His hand. And Joshua went to Him and said to Him, "Are You for us or for our adversaries?" So He said, "No, but as Commander of the army of the Lord I have now come." And Joshua fell on his face to the earth and worshiped, and said to Him, "What does my Lord say to His servant?"*
>
> JOSHUA 5:13-14

Notice Joshua's instant submission and humility to the LORD. He was willing to do whatever He instructed. It was as if the LORD was telling him, "Joshua, you are not going to lead the battle; I am here to lead the battle."

Think about what the LORD told Joshua next: *Then the Commander of the Lord's army said to Joshua, "Take your sandal off your foot, for the place where you stand is holy."*

And Joshua did so (Joshua 5:15). Where have we heard of this before? Moses, at the place of the burning bush was also told to take off his sandals, for the same reason—interesting. Every time the LORD dealt with His people and they sensed the holiness of God, we find them on the floor, head between their knees, as a symbol of servanthood. Joshua could go out to battle because he was now submitted to the Lordship of Jesus Christ. The LORD instructed Joshua how to defeat the city of Jericho. He was not going to use his nearly forty thousand men with spears and swords to fight (Joshua 4:13).

Joshua and the Lord's army were to march around it once, for six days, as seven priests bearing seven trumpets of rams' horns would go before the ark. On the seventh day they were to march around Jericho seven times, the priests were to blow the rams' horns, and the people were to shout with a great shout and the walls would fall down flat. Joshua after listening to the Commander of the LORD, might have said to himself, *Sure LORD?* His warriors of war might have thought Joshua had gone crazy!

Think about what the people living in Jericho thought, as they watched from the wall, while Joshua's army quietly walked around the city, day after day. They were commanded not to speak until the seventh day when they would shout and God would knock the walls down flat. Think about God's incredible strategy!

COUNTING THE COST

When we submit to Jesus Christ, and we turn from the world, we will have to count the cost. When we choose to follow Christ, we choose the cross, an instrument of death to self. Jesus told His followers: *"And whoever does not bear his cross and come after Me cannot be My disciple"* (Luke 14:27). Jesus is our ultimate example in counting the cost; he was mocked, spit upon, beaten and crucified. He is our Master—our King. As His followers, we have to be willing to walk in His footsteps and accept the same treatment. The only way to follow Christ is self-denial. Are you willing to do that? Are you willing to count the cost?

When you start attending church, and you begin to get to know Christ, I guarantee you will be hit from the enemy in every area of your life. At times, you are going to be discouraged, and the truth of God will be challenged, but you do not have to be afraid.

As we go through the Scriptures and see the spiritual battles different men and women faced, keep in mind, their stories were written for our example. Romans 15:4 exhorts us: *For whatever things were written before were written for our learning, that we through the patience and comfort of the Scriptures might have hope.* The servants of the Lord in the Old Testament and Christ's followers in the New Testament are constant examples. The main thing we have to understand is that this spiritual battle is real. If the believers in the Bible faced spiritual battles, then we must realize that we will also face the same. Whether they show us how they stood against their enemies, or even why they were defeated in the battle, we can learn from their lives—fully and completely.

Understand that following Jesus Christ does not keep us from suffering; but as Christians, we suffer for Christ's sake. We go through difficulties and even great trials, but the Lord is in control. The Apostle Paul, who suffered many trials, encouraged believers in Romans 8:31, when he said: ... *If God is for us, who can be against us?* Paul further reasoned with us:

> *Who shall separate us from the love of Christ? Shall tribulation, or distress, or persecution, or famine, or nakedness, or peril, or sword? As it is written: "For Your sake we are killed all day long; we are accounted as sheep for the slaughter."*
>
> ROMANS 8:35-36

Notice—nothing can separate us from the love of Christ, not even death—you always have Jesus Christ.

DENY YOURSELF

In our society today, the idea of denying ourselves anything is considered ludicrous. The world no longer recognizes moral absolutes, so we have gone back to the days of the Book of Judges, when the people no longer walked with the Lord or followed His ways. Judges 17:6 describes the ungodly attitude that was prevalent: *In those days there was no king in Israel; everyone did what was right in his own eyes.* Just like the children of Israel, people today do what is good in their own eyes. They focus on themselves and feed their fleshly desires. Multitudes of people follow the course of the world, but that direction leads to complete and utter destruction (Matthew 7:13-14).

Unfortunately, I am not just talking about those who follow the world. There are many Christians who stray from the *narrow path*; they are losing their own spiritual war. Why? Usually it is because they are unwilling to deny their flesh or turn away from the world. They become carnal Christians, and so many continue to become casualties in the war.

If we want to be victorious in this life, we need to listen to Jesus and do what He tells us. You have become a disciple of Jesus Christ; denial is the crux of a Christian called to spiritual warfare. Jesus taught his disciples: *"If anyone desires to come after Me, let him deny himself, and take up his cross, and follow Me"* (Matthew 16:24).

There are a great many correlations to spiritual warfare that, as a Christian, you can now identify with Christ. You will not carry a military pack, but a cross. Think about His words and what it means to deny yourself and take up your cross. The Roman cross was an instrument of torture and death. Jesus is calling each one of us to follow in His footsteps. The religious leaders beat Him; they spat on Him and nailed Him to a cross. Jesus could have stopped the Roman soldiers at any time, but He allowed His crucifixion. He denied His human desires and endured the pain of the cross. Jesus Christ is asking you to deny yourself and, if necessary, endure persecution or even death—martyrdom.

Paul the Apostle really understood and lived the teachings of Jesus Christ. He denied his human desires and endured tremendous persecution as he preached the message of the Gospel. He gave his testimony of persecution to the church of Corinth:

> From the Jews five times I received forty stripes minus one. Three times I was beaten with rods; once I was stoned; three times I was shipwrecked; a night and a day I have been in the deep; in journeys often, in perils of waters, in perils of robbers, in perils of my own countrymen, in perils of the Gentiles, in perils in the city, in perils in the wilderness, in perils in the sea, in perils among false brethren . . .
>
> 2 CORINTHIANS 11:24-26

When Paul wrote this second letter to the Corinthian church, he was not boasting or looking for pity. He was writing to them because they had accepted carnality. He wanted them to understand what it took to walk with Christ. He knew they would never be able to withstand the enemy in this spiritual battle, unless they denied their flesh. Before he ever gave his testimony of persecution, he spoke to them in his first letter about how he submitted to the Lord. Paul had to deny his flesh so God could use him: *But I discipline my body and bring it into subjection, lest, when I have preached to others, I myself should become disqualified* (1 Corinthians 9:27).

These Epistles were written to the Corinthian church because they were a carnal church and we have these letters to read today to exhort us. As Christians, we are called to lives of obedience, not carnality. God has provided us everything we need to protect ourselves against the enemy. He has equipped us for the spiritual battle we are in, but if we do not deny our flesh—carnal appetites—and turn from the things of this world, we will not have victory. If we allow our carnal desires and the world to control our lives, Satan will use these enemies against us. In the end, we will be fighting—the world, the flesh and the Devil all at one time. If we want to have victory in the spiritual battle, we have to defeat them through the power of the Holy Spirit that has been given to us.

Chapter 6

EMPOWERED FOR COMBAT

*"But you shall receive power when the Holy Spirit
has come upon you; and you shall be witnesses to Me
in Jerusalem, and in all Judea and Samaria, and
to the end of the earth."*
ACTS 1:8

Marines are handed their weaponry and given the necessary training for warfare, but it is up to them to combine their knowledge, strength, and courage, as they take action against their enemies. As a fully trained Marine and student in the art of Kung Fu San Soo, I had become a military killing machine. Early in life, I had learned to be empowered by my anger—in war it was fully unleashed.

On the battlefield I witnessed my friends being torn apart and killed, and this fueled my anger even more. It became such a deep-rooted anger that it drove me to the point where I needed help. After threatening my platoon leader, I ended up in a psych unit for six months. Amazingly, I was honorably discharged to return home.

When I married my wife Sharon, I still carried a lot of anger, and at times, it was triggered, even by something simple. When that happened, I acted violently toward my wife. Yet, I did not want to lose her.

I was tormented thinking she would leave me and take my boys. So, I made the decision to kill her and the kids, and I planned to die in a shoot-out with the police—my life would end in a fury of anger and violence. As I prepared, pacing and destroying everything in sight in my home, I hit the TV with the butt of my gun. The TV turned on and Pastor Chuck Smith was just smiling and preaching the Word of God. As I listened, the power of the Holy Spirit broke through me, and I asked Christ to forgive me and come into my life. The Word of God had more power than my anger. Seriously, I have never been the same since the Holy Spirit filled me with peace, and began to take control of my life—fully and completely.

No matter what we face in life, whether it is a battle with the world, the flesh, or Satan and his demons, we need the Holy Spirit if we want to be victorious. In spiritual warfare you have to be filled and empowered by the Holy Spirit; you cannot be empowered by anything else. The Lord has provided spiritual power and every piece of spiritual weaponry in order for the Christian to engage in spiritual warfare. Yet, if we are not empowered by the Spirit of God, we will be defeated.

I have counseled many times with people who are utterly defeated—it is so sad. Imagine all the people who feel overcome and not victorious. Some are not even willing to admit that their circumstances have defeated them. There are hundreds and thousands of believers in the body of Christ, all defeated. It sounds impossible, but it is the truth. Why? They can have all the head knowledge about God and the armor He provides, but without the power of the Holy Spirit in their lives, they will be defeated by their enemies.

JESUS AND HIS FOLLOWERS EMPOWERED

Jesus in the Wilderness

When Jesus was led of the Holy Spirit—driven into the wilderness—after 40 days of fasting, Satan tempted Him. Jesus won the spiritual battle with Satan in the wilderness because He was filled with the Holy Spirit. He went in the Spirit's might, and was led by the Spirit (Luke 4:1). Jesus used the Sword of the Spirit—God's Word—against Satan's attacks effectively (Luke 4:4-12). Jesus' victorious return to Galilee is described in Luke 4:14: *Then Jesus returned in the power of the Spirit to Galilee, and news of Him went out through all the surrounding region.*

He departed from the wilderness and continued to minister to the people in Galilee and the surrounding communities, by the power of the Holy Spirit. Knowing this, we must understand our great need for the power of the Spirit in our own lives. Jesus told His disciples who were in training for ministry: *"But you shall receive power when the Holy Spirit has come upon you..." (Acts 1:8).*

As you go through the Bible, it becomes clear that those who had victory in trials, tribulations, temptations and persecution were those who were empowered by the Spirit. They were not able to withstand the attacks of the enemy in their own strength. They were only able to beat their enemies through the power of the Spirit of God. In fact, Zechariah 4:6 tells us this truth in the battles we will face: *"...Not by might nor by power, but by My Spirit," says the Lord of hosts.*

The Apostles

As Jesus was empowered by the Holy Spirit, He promised His disciples they would also be empowered by Him. When Jesus departed to heaven, He commanded His disciples:

> *...not to depart from Jerusalem, but to wait for the Promise of the Father "which," He said, "you have heard from Me; for John truly baptized with water, but you shall be baptized with the Holy Spirit not many days from now"*
>
> ACTS 1:4-5

The disciples would receive Jesus' power in order to go out and be witnesses of Him, as they preached the Gospel. Jesus told them: *But you shall receive power when the Holy Spirit has come upon you; and you shall be witnesses to Me in Jerusalem, and in all Judea and Samaria, and to the end of the earth"* (Acts 1:8).

Jesus knew His disciples would face great persecution, and Satan would strongly come against them. He knew and understood the importance of the Holy Spirit in the life of the believer. His disciples, as *apostles,* which means "sent out ones," would need the power of the Holy Spirit to have victory in this spiritual battle.

After Jesus departed, He had the disciples wait together in an upper room in Jerusalem, and on the Day of Pentecost, the Holy Spirit was sent to empower them:

> *When the Day of Pentecost had fully come, they were all with one accord in one place. And suddenly there came a sound from heaven, as of a rushing mighty wind, and it filled the whole house where they were sitting. Then there appeared to them divided tongues, as of fire, and one sat upon each of them. And they were all filled with the Holy Spirit and began to speak with other tongues, as the Spirit gave them utterance.*
>
> ACTS 2:1-4

Immediately after the power of the Spirit came upon them, Peter stood up and preached the Gospel—the birth, death and resurrection of Christ—to the multitude gathered for Pentecost in Jerusalem. Pentecost was 50 days after the Sabbath of Passover, and in Judaism, it is called the Feast of Weeks. It was traditionally kept by Jewish men, who traveled to the city of Jerusalem as written in Deuteronomy 16:16. Peter, filled with the power of the Holy Spirit, stood before these multitudes, delivered to them the message of the Gospel, and called the people to repentance. About three thousand came to the Lord on that day (Acts 2:41).

Later, in Acts 4, Peter and John became prime targets. They were both arrested for preaching the death and resurrection of Jesus. The religious leaders did not want to hear or receive the message or accept the responsibility for putting the Messiah to death on the cross. When questioned about the healing of a lame man in Acts 3:1-3, they wanted to know by what power or by what name they had healed him.

Once again, the Holy Spirit empowered Peter to speak boldly to the Sanhedrin:

> *Then Peter, filled with the Holy Spirit, said to them, "Rulers of the people and elders of Israel: let it be known to you all, and to all the people of Israel, that by the name of Jesus Christ of Nazareth, whom you crucified, whom God raised from the dead, by Him this man stands here before you whole. This is the 'stone which was rejected by you builders, which has become the chief cornerstone.' Nor is there salvation in any other, for there is no other name under heaven given among men by which we must be saved."*
>
> ACTS 4:8, 10-12

After Peter spoke, the religious leaders forbade Peter and John to preach in the name of Jesus (Acts 4:18). However, despite persecution, they prayed to the Lord for boldness, and God answered them: *And when they had prayed, the place where they were assembled together was shaken; and they were all filled with the Holy Spirit, and they spoke the word of God with boldness* (Acts 4:31).

The Apostles continued their ministry among the people. They did many signs and wonders, and the sick and those brought to them with unclean spirits were all healed (Acts 5:12-16). For a second time, the Apostles were arrested, but on this occasion they were beaten. Once again they were forbidden to preach in the name of Jesus (Acts 5:40).

Notice, through the power of the Holy Spirit, their reaction to the persecution:

So they departed from the presence of the council, rejoicing that they were counted worthy to suffer shame for His name. And daily in the temple, and in every house, they did not cease teaching and preaching Jesus as the Christ.
ACTS 5:41-42

The religious leaders imprisoned the disciples more than once and threatened them with even greater punishment for preaching the death and resurrection of Jesus Christ, but they could not be stopped. They were filled with the Holy Spirit, and, through His power, they were able to overcome the trials and persecution they experienced.

Stephen Martyred

As many people were being added to the Church daily, great needs arose (Acts 2:46-47). There were not enough leaders to minister to the necessities of the people. The Apostles' priority was to minister to the people through the teaching of the Word, so it was necessary to bring up additional church leaders:

> Then the twelve summoned the multitude of the disciples and said, "It is not desirable that we should leave the Word of God and serve tables. Therefore, brethren, seek out from among you seven men of good reputation, full of the Holy Spirit and wisdom, whom we may appoint over this business."
>
> ACTS 6:2-3

Notice the qualifications needed to be a leader in the church. They had to be, "...of good reputation, and full of the Holy Spirit and wisdom." Not only is it impossible to minister without the Holy Spirit, but it is not possible to be a leader and engage in spiritual battles without Him.

Stephen was among the seven men selected, and he was a man full of the Holy Spirit: *And they chose Stephen, a man full of faith and the Holy Spirit, and Philip, Prochorus, Nicanor, Timon, Parmenas, and Nicolas, a proselyte from Antioch* (Acts 6:5).

Men arose from the synagogue and disputed with Stephen: *And they were not able to resist the wisdom and the Spirit by which he spoke* (Acts 6:10).

Before he was ever selected to serve in the ministry, God knew the great battles Stephen would face. Stephen would be called on to preach the Gospel, as false accusations of blasphemy were brought against him. This would be his final battle:

They also set up false witnesses who said, "This man does not cease to speak blasphemous words against this holy place and the law; for we have heard him say that this Jesus of Nazareth will destroy this place and change the customs which Moses delivered to us."

ACTS 6:13-14

Stephen was under attack from the enemy, and he did not have time to go back and arm himself. He had to be ready with the full armor of God, and he had to be empowered by the Holy Spirit. He was on his own, and the enemy wanted to defeat him. In Acts 7:1, as he faced the council, they confronted him: *Then the high priest said, "Are these things so?"*

Stephen, being filled with the Holy Spirit, proceeded to preach the Gospel message to the religious people who wanted to defeat him. In a long discourse in Acts 7:2-53, Stephen took them through the history of Israel, pointing out the many times they rebelled against the Lord. In the end, he pointed out their greatest sin:

"You stiff-necked and uncircumcised in heart and ears! You always resist the Holy Spirit; as your fathers did, so do you. Which of the prophets did your fathers not persecute? And

they killed those who foretold the coming of the Just One, of whom you now have become the betrayers and murderers, who have received the law by the direction of angels and have not kept it."

ACTS 7:51-53

They had resisted the Holy Spirit, killed the prophets, and murdered the Messiah. They received the Law of God but failed to keep it.

Imagine the power behind Stephen, what it took for him to face his enemies and point out their sin for all to hear. Stephen was in a spiritual battle, and he could not face the enemy without the Holy Spirit's power. He knew he was at their mercy, but he did not fail to stand with the Lord and engage the enemy in battle.

When he finished, his accusers were so angry, they ran at him, cast him out of the city and stoned him. They knew they were guilty, and they did not want to hear what Stephen was saying. They could have repented, but they chose to kill him instead.

Many would look at this and think that Stephen lost the spiritual war, but he did not. Stephen finished his race well and he was taken up to heaven:

But he, being full of the Holy Spirit, gazed into heaven and saw the glory of God, and Jesus standing at the right hand of God, and said, "Look! I see the heavens opened and the Son of

Man standing at the right hand of God!"

ACTS 7:55-56

And they stoned Stephen as he was calling on God and saying, "Lord Jesus, receive my spirit." Then he knelt down and cried out with a loud voice, "Lord, do not charge them with this sin." And when he had said this, he fell asleep.

ACTS 7:59-60

Paul's Spiritual Warfare

When we talk about spiritual warfare and the empowering of the Holy Spirit, we cannot leave out the life of Paul the Apostle. He was a man who was transformed by the grace of God and empowered by the Holy Spirit to preach the Gospel of Jesus Christ to the Gentiles. Because of his background as a Pharisee, a member of the Sanhedrin and a persecutor of Christians, Paul experienced great trials, tribulations, temptations and persecution in his life. He had many enemies, and they numbered themselves among Gentiles and Jews alike.

In the Book of 2 Corinthians, Paul, in defense of accusations from false prophets, listed the number of persecutions he endured as he sought to serve the Lord:

Are they Hebrews? So am I. Are they Israelites? So am I. Are they the seed of Abraham? So am I. Are they ministers of Christ?—I speak as a fool—I am more: in labors more abundant, in stripes above measure, in prisons more frequently, in deaths often. From the Jews five times I received

*forty stripes minus one. Three times I was beaten with rods;
once I was stoned; three times I was shipwrecked; a night and
a day I have been in the deep; in journeys often, in perils of
waters, in perils of robbers, in perils of my own countrymen,
in perils of the Gentiles, in perils in the city, in perils in the
wilderness, in perils in the sea, in perils among false brethren;
in weariness and toil, in sleeplessness often, in hunger and
thirst, in fastings often, in cold and nakedness—*

2 CORINTHIANS 11:22-27

Look at the physical battles Paul endured as he went out to
serve the Lord. He truly knew he was in a spiritual battle, and
he knew he needed the empowering of the Holy Spirit in order
to have victory. There is no way he could have endured the
extreme physical persecution without the Holy Spirit. If he had
tried to do it in his own power, he would have been defeated.

As Paul was empowered by the Holy Spirit, he was also
led by Him. He made three missionary journeys, and all were
led by the Holy Spirit who called him out for the work of the
ministry. He guided Paul from one city to the next:

*As they ministered to the Lord and fasted, the Holy Spirit
said, "Now separate to Me Barnabas and Saul for the work
to which I have called them" So, being sent out by the Holy
Spirit, they went down to Seleucia, and from there they sailed
to Cyprus. And when they arrived in Salamis, they preached
the word of God in the synagogues of the Jews. They also had
John as their assistant.*

ACTS 13:2, 4-5

In Acts 21:4, the Holy Spirit warned Paul to avoid Jerusalem, but later told him what awaited him when he got to Jerusalem:

When he had come to us, he took Paul's belt, bound his own hands and feet, and said, "Thus says the Holy Spirit, 'So shall the Jews at Jerusalem bind the man who owns this belt, and deliver him into the hands of the Gentiles'"
ACTS 21:11

Paul's intimate experience and knowledge of spiritual warfare was used to encourage Christians to endure. Paul wrote to the Ephesian church and told them to put on the full armor of God in order to combat Satan and his demons: *Put on the whole armor of God, that you may be able to stand against the wiles of the devil* (Ephesians 6:11).

Knowing how he battled against his own flesh, he told the Corinthian church how to subdue the flesh. In 1 Corinthians 9:27 he told them: *But I discipline my body and bring it into subjection, lest, when I have preached to others, I myself should become disqualified.*

Just as he warned against Satan and the flesh, Paul told the Galatian churches they needed Christ to be their Redeemer from this world:

Even so we, when we were children, were in bondage under the elements of the world. But when the fullness of the time had come, God sent forth His Son, born of a woman, born

*under the law, to redeem those who were under the law, that
we might receive the adoption as sons.*

GALATIANS 4:3-5

CHRISTIANS EMPOWERED

As you go through your Bible, from the Old Testament to the New Testament, you see that the Spirit's power was essential for God's people to have victory over their enemies. Many of the people in the Bible, such as Samson, David and Peter, were at times, defeated by their flesh and had to learn this important lesson the hard way. But God ministered to His people and empowered them to serve Him and withstand the attacks of the enemy, through the power of the Holy Spirit. Without the Spirit, not one of the men and women in the Bible would have been victorious. They would have all been casualties in the war.

Holy men of God were moved by the Spirit of God to write the Word of God:

*And so we have the prophetic word confirmed, which you
do well to heed as a light that shines in a dark place, until
the day dawns and the morning star rises in your hearts;
knowing this first, that no prophecy of Scripture is of any
private interpretation, for prophecy never came by the will
of man, but holy men of God spoke as they were moved by
the Holy Spirit.*

2 PETER 1:19-21

These men endured great trials and tribulations to bring us the Word of God, and they did it with great joy, knowing their LORD, their reward, was in heaven. Paul had endured much affliction, but he kept the joy of the Holy Spirit in his life. He wrote to the Thessalonians:

For our gospel did not come to you in word only, but also in power, and in the Holy Spirit and in much assurance, as you know what kind of men we were among you for your sake. And you became followers of us and of the Lord, having received the word in much affliction, with joy of the Holy Spirit.

1 THESSALONIANS 1:5-6

Knowing the heavy price many men paid in order to give us the Word of God, we should be diligent to read and study it, so we are prepared for the spiritual warfare we will encounter in our lives. God gave us His Word and the examples of His people, so we can better understand our enemy when assaulted.

WALK IN THE SPIRIT

When we learn to die to ourselves, to our fleshly desires, then we can follow Jesus Christ. Paul wrote to the churches in Galatia, telling them to deny the flesh and walk according to the Spirit of God. He told them:

Walk in the Spirit, and you shall not fulfill the lust of the flesh. For the flesh lusts against the Spirit, and the Spirit against

*the flesh; and these are contrary to one another, so that you
do not do the things that you wish.*
GALATIANS 5:16-17

Paul did not just exhort them to walk in the Spirit, but they needed to examine their lives for any evidence of the flesh:

*Now the works of the flesh are evident, which are: adultery,
fornication, uncleanness, lewdness, idolatry, sorcery, hatred,
contentions, jealousies, outbursts of wrath, selfish ambitions,
dissensions, heresies, envy, murders, drunkenness, revelries,
and the like; of which I tell you beforehand, just as I also told
you in time past, that those who practice such things will not
inherit the kingdom of God.*
GALATIANS 5:19-21

When we examine our lives we should be able to determine if we are denying the flesh or indulging it.

In the same way, there is also evidence to see if we are walking in the Spirit, since *the fruit of the Spirit is love, joy, peace, longsuffering, kindness, goodness, faithfulness, gentleness, self-control. Against such there is no law* (Galatians 5:22-23).

If we say we are Christians and we are walking with Christ, we should see evidence of that spiritual life—the fruit of the Spirit.

Whether you choose to be honest with yourself or not, the evidence is there for all to see. If you are walking in the

Spirit, you will have victory in this spiritual war we are in. If you are walking in the flesh, you will be defeated, and if you make a practice of the sins mentioned in Galatians 5:19-21, you will not inherit the kingdom of God. It is important to heed that warning.

Seriously, because I love you, and I want you to have victory in Christ, I exhort you, just as Paul exhorted the churches in Galatians 5:24-26:

> And those who are Christ's have crucified the flesh with its passions and desires. If we live in the Spirit, let us also walk in the Spirit. Let us not become conceited, provoking one another, envying one another.

Then again in, Romans 8:12-13, notice how Paul urges us to put to death our flesh, by the power of the Spirit within us:

> Therefore, brethren, we are debtors—not to the flesh, to live according to the flesh. For if you live according to the flesh you will die; but if by the Spirit you put to death the deeds of the body, you will live.

SPIRIT-FILLED COMRADES

Some of the strongest relationships I have built are with men who fought with me on the frontlines in Vietnam. We could count on our comrades to be there when we needed each other the most. If injured in combat, we knew we would carry each other out. If necessary, we were ready to give our lives for one another on the battlefield, we would leave no man behind.

Israel entered into a battle with one of their main enemies—Amalek. Moses, their leader, held the rod of God, and lifted up his hands during this long battle. When his arms grew tired, other men had to support his hands. Exodus 17:8-13 tells us of this battle:

> *Now Amalek came and fought with Israel in Rephidim. And Moses said to Joshua, "Choose us some men and go out, fight with Amalek. Tomorrow I will stand on the top of the hill with the rod of God in my hand." So Joshua did as Moses said to him, and fought with Amalek. And Moses, Aaron, and Hur went up to the top of the hill. And so it was, when Moses held up his hand, that Israel prevailed; and when he let down his hand, Amalek prevailed. But Moses' hands became heavy; so they took a stone and put it under him, and he sat on it. And Aaron and Hur supported his hands, one on one side, and the other on the other side; and his hands were steady until the going down of the sun. So Joshua defeated Amalek and his people with the edge of the sword.*

If Moses' hands had not been lifted up by these godly men, the people of Israel would have been defeated in the battle!

Spiritually speaking, in Scripture, Amalek is symbolic of the flesh. During spiritual warfare, we certainly need our hands raised up in prayer, or we, too, shall be defeated. If Moses needed his hands lifted up, how much more do we? We all need friends and co-workers in our lives to hold up our arms. There are those men and women who are called by God and empowered by the Holy Spirit to fight the battle with you!

In the body of Christ as people go through different problems and situations, I have observed many defeats. Often, because of pride, we keep the battles we are going through private. Yet we have comrades in Christ, in whom we can confide. We do not even have to share all the specifics, but understand, the body of Christ is our family, and they are willing to pray for us. The enemy tries to take advantage of us, but we must fight this spiritual battle on our knees with other spirit filled believers. God has placed us together for a reason so that we can pray and encourage each other.

David had been anointed by the prophet Samuel to be the next king of Israel: *and the Spirit of the Lord came upon him from that day forward* (1 Samuel 16:13). Before he became king, David had a loyal friendship with Jonathan, King Saul's son—the King of Israel. David and Jonathan became close comrades:

Now when he [David] *had finished speaking to Saul, the soul of Jonathan was knit to the soul of David, and Jonathan loved him as his own soul. Saul took him* [David] *that day, and would not let him go home to his father's house anymore. Then Jonathan and David made a covenant, because he loved him as his own soul. And Jonathan took off the robe that was on him and gave it to David, with his armor, even to his sword and his bow and his belt. So David went out wherever Saul sent him, and behaved wisely. And Saul set him over the men of war, and he was accepted in the sight of all the people and also in the sight of Saul's servants.*

1 SAMUEL 18:1-5

David was in favor with God and the people, but after King Saul became jealous of him, he had to flee. He remained in the cave of Adullam, where men who were loyal to the Spirit anointed king, gathered to him, and they became his mighty men of valor. These men faithfully fought alongside him on the battlefield, and their hearts became knit together:

David therefore departed from there and escaped to the cave of Adullam. So when his brothers and all his father's house heard it, they went down there to him. And everyone who was in distress, everyone who was in debt, and everyone who was discontented gathered to him. So he became captain over them. And there were about four hundred men with him.

1 SAMUEL 22: 1-2

In the New Testament, you will notice other close friendships that are spiritually empowered. The Apostle Paul had a faithful friend Luke; he was a physician who stood by Paul, even when others had deserted him. Paul, in prison in Rome, wrote a final letter to Timothy—his son in the Christian faith—and said: *Only Luke is with me* (2 Timothy 4:11).

Priscilla and Aquila were Paul's co-workers in the ministry. Like Paul, they were tentmakers by trade. In times of persecution, they risked their necks for him. In a greeting to the Romans, Paul wrote:

Greet Priscilla and Aquila, my fellow workers in Christ Jesus, who risked their own necks for my life, to whom not only I give thanks, but also all the churches of the Gentiles.

ROMANS 16:3-4

Men and women of old have fought and won the battles of the Lord by His Spirit. Believers around the world today are empowered, by the Spirit of God, to carry out great exploits for the Lord, as they stand firm against the flesh, the world, Satan and his demons.

Chapter 7

GOD OUR PROTECTOR

I will lift up my eyes to the hills—from whence comes my
help? My help comes from the Lord, who made heaven
and earth. He will not allow your foot to be moved;
He who keeps you will not slumber.
PSALM 121:1-3

Ironically, in Vietnam, I noticed there were no atheists in the foxholes—makeshift pits, dug by Marines for a defensive fighting position. As we took in fire from the enemy, I often saw Marines do the sign of the cross, while they prayerfully asked God to protect them in the battle.

Reflecting back to the battles in Vietnam, there were so many occasions when I should have been killed. I could tell you story after story of how my life was protected. I remember one time when I was walking point out of a village; the enemy soldiers had me in their sights. They fired. Bullets ripped through the air, and the 50 caliber rounds ricocheted down by my feet. Immediately, I jumped for cover and remained pinned down. I knew if these 50 calibers hit, everything would disappear! I remained hidden underneath the dykes by the rice paddies, until help arrived.

During another attack, bullets from an AK-44 assault rifle were literally flying all over me. Some bullets directly hit my back and knocked me down. Even though I could feel the intense burn throughout my whole back, the bullet did not go through; I was protected by my flack gear.

Another time, leaving a village at night, I was training a young 18-year-old from Texas how to walk point. We hustled through the first bamboo gate, and we were ok. After the second gate, he tripped a wire. I tried to push him, but the blast got all of us, and we went flying. There was a fire fight going on, so the helicopters could not come down. We were pinned down for seven hours in the night, firing against the Viet Cong. Both the young man's legs were gone, and his right arm was blown off. I was hit, but I did not know it until I stood up to fire back at the enemy; I felt dizzy, and collapsed. Soon enough, I was flown by Medevac out of danger and taken to the hospital.

Another time, while walking point, I routinely jumped a fence. Suddenly, an undetected bomb triggered, and the force of its blast threw me backwards—airborne. I suffered minor injuries, but incredibly, once again my life was saved.

Later on, when I surrendered my life to the Lord, I realized, for sure, God had protected me on the battlefields of Vietnam. I still have shrapnel imbedded in my body. All my battle scars and wounds serve as a constant reminder of how God spared my life, so many times. I should have been the one who died, but God had a purpose for my life. God is good. Truly, it is a miracle—I should not be here.

More importantly, as a Christian, I understood that I was engaged in a tremendous spiritual battle. This was certainly a very different kind of warfare. But God, through the many difficulties I had faced during the Vietnam War, would show me how to use those experiences to help me fight the spiritual warfare I would face as a Christian.

Imagine, God had an ultimate plan to use my training as a Marine, as well as everything He had allowed me to go through in battle, for good. Eventually, as I became a pastor, the Lord would equip me in that call, using His spiritual weaponry to fight a spiritual battle. I was called to be on the front lines, leading and ministering to His precious people—amazing!

Help for King Hezekiah

Among the kings of Israel, King Hezekiah did what was right in the sight of the Lord. He began his reign over Judah in the city of Jerusalem at 25. He followed in the footsteps of his predecessor, King David (2 Kings 18:1-3). Hezekiah was not like the rest of God's people who had chosen to make gods out of wooden images. They had even taken the bronze serpent Moses had formed in the wilderness and burned incense to it. Hezekiah broke in pieces the bronze serpent and removed idolatry from Judah (2 Kings 18:4).

Hezekiah listened to the warnings of God and set about to keep the commandments which the Lord had commanded Moses. King Hezekiah trusted the Lord. As king, he depended on the teachings of God's Word and clung to His promises (2 Kings 5-6).

King Hezekiah wanted to get close to the heart of God, to know His heart and mind. He had persevered in hard times, because the Lord was with him (2 Kings 18:7-8).

Then, the King of Assyria besieged Samaria, and after three long years, he was able to seize the land. The northern part of Israel was taken captive. Under the reign of Hoshea, King of Israel, the people fell into captivity, because they did not obey God's commands or obey His voice (2 Kings 17; 18:9-12).

The Assyrians had the worst reputation in warfare. Most nations who faced battle with the Assyrians, rather than being taken captive, preferred to commit suicide. They knew of the brutal atrocities the Assyrians committed against their captives. Prisoners were stripped in order to shame them. Every person, including women and children, was separated from their families. The Assyrians dismembered their captives. They would systematically cut off a hand, a toe or a tongue. Hot irons were stuck into their eyes to make them blind or cruelly shoved up their noses. Other captives were taken and buried alive up to their mouths or noses and left to slowly suffocate.

Mercilessly, some of their captives were skinned alive, impaled on stakes, beheaded or even set on fire. Those who survived the Assyrians' ruthlessness had a hole drilled through their nose, lip or ear. Then a hook attached to a chain was placed through that hole and used to drag them off into captivity.

During the invasion, the Assyrians left some of the poor people of Israel behind. They remained in the land and intermarried with the Assyrians. These people later became the Samaritans, who were treated with contempt and hatred by the Jews who had pure ancestry because they were considered to be half breeds.

Then, eight years later, after the attack on Samaria, King Sennacherib of Assyria began to attack and take control of all the fortified cities of Judah. At that time, Hezekiah used wisdom to make peaceful negotiations with the Assyrians. A tribute of silver was given to Sennacherib from the king's rich treasuries, and gold was stripped from the doors of the temple and pillars (2 Kings 18:13-16).

Sennacherib, confident in himself and his exploits, ordered a siege against Jerusalem. His pride rose up, and just like Satan, this ruthless king enticed the people. Sennacherib used scare tactics against the people of Jerusalem. He sent the leaders of his great army, to question the validity of King Hezekiah's trust in God. These men of war tried to discourage the people in an attempt to make them rebel against Hezekiah. They threatened the people as if to say, "We want you and your children to place your trust in our god. If you do not—there will be consequences" (2 Kings 18:17-30).

However, if the people yielded to King Sennacherib's demands and chose to place their trust in him, then this heathen king would offer to roll out the red carpet to them:

"Do not listen to Hezekiah; for thus says the king of Assyria: 'Make peace with me by a present and come out to me; and every one of you eat from his own vine and every one from his own fig tree, and every one of you drink the waters of his own cistern; until I come and take you away to a land like your own land, a land of grain and new wine, a land of bread and

vineyards, a land of olive groves and honey, that you may live and not die. But do not listen to Hezekiah, lest he persuade you, saying, 'The Lord will deliver us.'"

2 KINGS 18:31-32

Sennacherib continued to be like Satan, just as we later see the Devil testing Jesus in (Matthew 4:3-11). He used the same tactics, "If you do as I request, then I will promise to give you rewards."

Sennacherib's leaders described their king's accomplishments, his great acts of war, as if Jerusalem was the next to be crushed. The Assyrians wanted the people of Jerusalem to live in fear, as if their destruction was imminent. Sennacherib mocked God and contradicted His Word, even to the point where he blasphemed. Sennacherib told the people in Jerusalem that he had personally heard from the Lord. He said the God of Israel had told Him to come against them. Help was futile; they should expect no help from their Egyptian allies or their own God. Within Sennacherib's message to the people, he continued to slander the character of Hezekiah. Why? It was a blatant attempt to break the people's trust in their king. Sennacherib's men tried to reason with and intimidate the people. Surely, if these other nations could not be delivered by their gods whom they had trusted in, then God could not deliver Jerusalem from Sennacherib's hand (2 Kings 18:33).

However, King Hezekiah, having foreseen this deception, had already instructed his people not to answer Sennacherib.

So, after their enemies had spoken, the people held their peace; they did not answer back a single word: *But the people held their peace and answered him not a word; for the king's commandment was, "Do not answer him"* (2 Kings 18:36).

Yet, as King Hezekiah's counselors returned, they were freaking out! They came to the king with their clothes torn as they gave him a letter from the King Sennacherib's messengers and told him all they had said (2 Kings 18:37; Isaiah 37:14).

This tricky situation, once again reminds me of when I was in Vietnam. We had to endure the constant threats and attempts of the enemy, as they tried to brainwash us. Our enemies tried to make us fearful. When we were out in the field, they were there with microphones saying, "Americans surrender; we will treat you well." They gave us empty promises—it was a bunch of baloney.

Christians should not be easily threatened. They should be able to discern what is true or false. Otherwise, believers can become swayed by the enemy's deception, and, out of fear, they can be tempted to disobey the Lord.

Seriously, when people come against me I say, "Get in line!" I say to myself, *Without God's permission they cannot hurt me. Give me a break!*

Maybe you are facing a real threat in your life, and you feel there is no light at the end of the tunnel. But God is there with you. Remember, I say again, if the Lord is for you, then who can be against you, right? As long as you and I are with God, He is with us. The day we leave the Lord, we are on our own. So we need to keep our trust in the Lord. I cannot deliver you, but God can.

As long as you and I are with God, He is with us.
The day we leave the Lord we are on our own.

Look at Hezekiah's response. Where did he go? He entered the temple to speak with the Lord. Even while Sennacherib and his army were still intimidating them, the king opened the letter containing their threats of captivity, and rolled it out before the Lord: *And Hezekiah received the letter from the hand of the messengers, and read it; and Hezekiah went up to the house of the Lord, and spread it before the Lord* (Isaiah 37:14).

Hezekiah recognized there was one, true God, and only He could help them. Hezekiah voiced a theological prayer, as he declared God to be the Creator:

Then Hezekiah prayed to the Lord, saying: "O Lord of hosts, God of Israel, the One who dwells between the cherubim, You are God, You alone, of all the kingdoms of the earth. You have made heaven and earth. Incline Your ear, O Lord, and hear; open Your eyes, O Lord, and see; and hear all the words of Sennacherib, which he has sent to reproach the living God.

Truly, Lord, the kings of Assyria have laid waste all the nations and their lands, and have cast their gods into the fire; for they were not gods, but the work of men's hands—wood and stone. Therefore they destroyed them. Now therefore, O Lord our God, save us from his hand, that all the kingdoms of the earth may know that You are the Lord, You alone."

ISAIAH 37:15-20

King Hezekiah's prayer was immediately heard. The answer came—I love it! Notice God's master plan—Hezekiah was prophesying. Prayer turned the tides of war, and the plans of the enemy would be turned around. The Lord would do the same thing to the Assyrians as they had done to their enemies—He would drive them away. Why does Hezekiah want to win the battle? Because he could show to all the other kingdoms of the earth that God is LORD over all!

Hezekiah could now go to bed and get a good night's sleep. The next morning, as he woke up and opened the window, guess what he saw? God's deliverance! The Assyrians lay dead all around. What had happened here? During the night, the LORD had sent one angel to kill 185,000 Assyrians. They were all dead. God's people were protected—it happened just as God's Word said it would.

What a great lesson for us! Where is the best place to go when you are in trouble? The house of the LORD! Why? In times of trouble, it is good to be in the house of God, because it becomes a place of refuge. The Church is a hospital for whatever your problems may be. It is a place where God protects us, forgives us, and speaks to us. When the pressure is on, take time to be with the LORD. Worship Him.

I believe with all my heart, we do not have to fear our enemy; we just have to pray and trust God. Listen, never take it personally when people are coming against you. They are mocking God and coming against Him. The LORD can turn around the tides of every battle if we would only pray to Him. We must spread our problems out before the LORD, pray, and then wait on Him to do a great work. However, we do have to get rid of all our idols—our lives need to be holy before the LORD.

Seeking God's Protection

In the Book of Psalms, we see the heart of David and the hearts of the different men who wrote these powerful Psalms. What they have written still speaks to our hearts today. Psalms 120-134 are known as *Psalms of Ascent*. As the Jews came to the great feasts—Passover, Pentecost and the Feast of Tabernacles—they traveled up to Jerusalem to worship the LORD. They came from all over the world. Jerusalem was situated in a good defensive position, as it was surrounded by mountains. The city was built on top of a mountain, 2,500 feet above sea level.

Psalm 121 is a Psalm written about God's help to those who seek Him. The psalmist begins to give us a full picture of the hilly country surrounding the city of Jerusalem. You have to understand, the psalmist was contemplating on Israel's backslidden state. Instead of worshiping the LORD, in the hills they worshiped idols—other gods.

Then the psalmist lifted up his eyes to the heavens, and as he looked up over the hills of Jerusalem, he said: *I will lift up my eyes to the hills— from whence comes my help?* He answered the question: *My help comes from the Lord, who made heaven and earth* (Psalm 121:1-2).

The psalmist spoke about the power of the true and living God. He did not speak about idols, for those who worship God must worship Him in Spirit and in truth (John 4:24). God is Creator—the Designer behind the design, creation. So incredible.

The Psalm continues: *He will not allow your foot to be moved; He who keeps you will not slumber. Behold, He who keeps Israel shall neither slumber nor sleep* (Psalm 121:3-4).

Whatever you are facing in your life, always remember, God is not sleeping; He is awake, 24/7—365 days a year! He is eternal. If you really seek God and call upon Him, He hears and listens. Surely, if you have problems, God will be there. The LORD is your help! Think about how the psalmist speaks to your own heart as we conclude the Psalm:

The Lord is your keeper; the Lord is your shade at your right hand. The sun shall not strike you by day, nor the moon by night. The Lord shall preserve you from all evil; He shall preserve your soul. The Lord shall preserve your going out and your coming in from this time forth, and even forevermore.

PSALM 121:5-8

It is so beautiful to see who the LORD had become to His people. He was their Keeper. When His people came from the desert area, there were no trees or shade. It was very hot. Yet they trusted in Yahweh—the great I AM, who, in their past history in the wilderness with Moses, gave His people water, meat and brought them shade. He protected them and gave them everything they needed.

The psalmist mentioned the *right hand*, because when those who were armed raised their sword or spear they exposed a vulnerable area on their bodies. The enemy looked for an opening to strike, and they could be killed very easily. On the left side their defense was the stronger because they were able to protect themselves by holding a shield.

God is our Provider and the Protector of our lives. He is our Shield—the One who goes before us, to keep us and watch over us. I think of how good God is to us—amazing—amazing!

A Soldier's Psalm

Psalm 91 is another interesting Psalm that speaks about the safety of abiding in the presence of God. The psalmist raises the question about how we are living. He causes us to come to a place of self-examination in our lives. He shows each of us who we are, and what we are, so we can see if we are living in accordance with the holiness of God.

> *He who dwells in the secret place of the Most High shall abide under the shadow of the Almighty. I will say of the Lord, "He is my refuge and my fortress; My God, in Him I will trust."*
> PSALM 91:1-2

In reference to the culture at that time, God's people fled up into the high tower to take refuge from the enemy. The enemy could not kill them there. The LORD became the High Tower to His people—a place with God where they felt safe.

As a Christian, it is important to understand that you need to abide in Jesus Christ, which means to *dwell* or to *stay* (John 15). There is no way that anyone can really experience the love and peace of God, unless they truly abide in the secret place of the LORD Most High. If you ever become depressed, read these verses. You can abide in the shadow of the Almighty— He is God.

> *Surely He shall deliver you from the snare of the fowler and from the perilous pestilence. He shall cover you with*

His feathers, and under His wings you shall take refuge; His truth shall be your shield and buckler.

PSALM 91:3-4

The *fowler* is used in reference to Satan. But also, the Hebrew word used is in reference to a person who sets traps to catch birds. In biblical times, they did not have shot guns to shoot the birds down. Instead, the people would set up nets that swept over a certain area. Then, as they would hit the branches, the birds would be startled and fly up into the nets. Their wings would get tangled. Then, the fowler easily caught, killed and ate them.

Interestingly, the word *snare* is also in reference to Satan, who sets up traps. We need to be careful about the traps Satan wants to ensnare us with—he is pretty smart. I do not think many of us have come up against Satan. He can only be in one place at one time, but all of us, at one time or another, have fought with demons.

Satan works hard and uses his captains, lieutenants and privates in his plans to do everything he can in his power to ensnare us, until the day we die. He is the Prince of this World, and the chief commander of his army. He gives his demons instructions and commands, as they try to ensnare us through different trials, temptations and oppression or depression.

While you sleep, Satan plans and sets up his nets. He tries to ensnare people by the sin in their life. Just like the birds that try to fly away and escape, they get trapped in the nets, set for them. Think about Christians who have become ensnared by their sins and become victims of Satan. Many people believe they will never fall, but that is pride, and they will fall for sure. If you do not keep yourself in the love of God every day, then you become a target. You never know when your weakness is going to be matched by the enemy.

Notice in Psalm 91:5-8, how God is our Refuge. We do not have to fear. We need to keep our eyes on the LORD. The wicked will be defeated:

You shall not be afraid of the terror by night, nor of the arrow that flies by day, nor of the pestilence that walks in darkness, nor of the destruction that lays waste at noonday a thousand may fall at your side, and ten thousand at your right hand; but it shall not come near you. Only with your eyes shall you look, and see the reward of the wicked.

I was not a Christian, but this Scripture became very real to my life. One night in Vietnam, we were up on Hill 55. The Vietnamese had come up over the hill—a whole platoon. Over a thousand Viet Cong were coming against us. They reached the barbed wire and climbed over. As they advanced they tripped off the mines, and the explosion blew up everything in sight.

We all knew it was not a good situation; we were caught by surprise. There were only 60 of us fighting to hold the hill. As the battle continued, you could see the streaks of red tracers, illuminated against the dark, night sky. Despite the fury of firefight, the Viet Cong still kept coming, closer and closer. Finally, the enemy entered the camp—we were overrun. I was engaged in hand-to-hand combat with the enemy, their guns and knives were up close to my face.

Then in the morning, still exhausted, I looked out over the desolate battlefield. Dead bodies were strewn across the land, and there lay my friends—dead. Instantly, the reality of life hit me hard . . . this war was real. Yet, astonishingly, from out of all those people who had died, I had survived. I should have been among those killed, but God protected me. God had spared my life, even though I was a heathen,

Because you have made the Lord, who is my refuge, even the Most High, your dwelling place, no evil shall befall you, nor shall any plague come near your dwelling; for He shall give His angels charge over you, to keep you in all your ways. In their hands they shall bear you up, lest you dash your foot against a stone. You shall tread upon the lion and the cobra, the young lion and the serpent you shall trample underfoot.

PSALM 91:9-13

These verses are incredible, because there is a two-fold interpretation. First, this is a prophecy of when Jesus Christ was being tempted by Satan in Matthew 4:5-6:

Then the devil took Him up into the holy city, set Him on the pinnacle of the temple, and said to Him, "If You are the Son of

God, throw Yourself down. For it is written: 'He shall give His angels charge over you,' and, 'In their hands they shall bear you up, lest you dash your foot against a stone.' "

Second, this is also in reference to God's angels who protect you and me. We have body guards behind us that watch over us day and night—amazing!

Notice how God keeps us from diseases—I like that! When I was in China, on a missionary journey, I was given rice, and as I ate, I uncovered the head of this rooster. It was stiff with its tongue sticking straight out at me! I was with Pastor Mike Macintosh, who got really freaked out! I was hungry and needed to eat. I am God's child, so I asked the Lord to bless the food and I ate. Seriously, I did not have to worry about diseases.

I really believe that if I am on a missionary journey in the jungles of Colombia, and I step on a cobra and it bites me, then, like Paul I believe I could shake it off and God would heal me (Acts 28:1-5). However, if God chooses not to heal me, then I will be in the presence of the Lord. I love that!

In the conclusion of Psalm 91 is God's promise of protection:

Because he has set his love upon Me, therefore I will deliver him; I will set him on high, because he has known My name. He shall call upon Me, and I will answer him; I will be with him in trouble; I will deliver him and honor him. With long life I will satisfy him, and show him My salvation.

PSALM 91:14-16

God protects us because He loves us. The blessings of obedience are a long life—your days will be extended. The Lord will cause you to be prosperous.

Jesus in the Storm

In the Book of Matthew, the disciples of Jesus experienced tremendous storms while they were on boats in the middle of the Sea of Galilee. During the first storm, Jesus was in the boat with them. Matthew 8:23-25 describes how the storm grew stronger, and the ferocious waves came into the boat:

> . . . *suddenly a great tempest arose on the sea, so that the boat was covered with the waves. But He was asleep. Then His disciples came to Him and awoke Him, saying, "Lord, save us! We are perishing!"*

When this storm came, Jesus was asleep. He did not wake up, even though the boat was being tossed about on the waves. Jesus was secure in the Father, but the disciples were afraid. In the middle of the storm, they panicked and woke Him up to save their lives. In Matthew 8:26-27 Jesus said to them:

> *"Why are you fearful, O you of little faith?" Then He arose and rebuked the winds and the sea, and there was a great calm. So the men marveled, saying, "Who can this be, that even the winds and the sea obey Him?"*

Jesus calmed the tempestuous wind and the sea. He brought peace in the middle of a storm. Notice that the disciples had awakened Jesus to save them, but when he did, they were astonished.

When we are going through an impossible trial, and when the situation is miraculously resolved, we are amazed! I think we act just like the disciples. We cannot believe the outcome, even though we have been praying for the Lord's assistance.

In the second storm, the disciples were sent out on the water without Jesus: *Immediately Jesus made His disciples get into the boat and go before Him to the other side, while He sent the multitudes away* (Matthew 14:22). They were once again in the middle of the Sea of Galilee when the storm came: *But the boat was now in the middle of the sea, tossed by the waves, for the wind was contrary* (Matthew 14:24).

In the first storm, Jesus was with His disciples. They were able to wake Him up to save them. This time, Jesus was not with them, but He knew what was happening to His disciples. They were in the middle of a storm, and their boat was being tossed about. Then Jesus came to them:

> *Now in the fourth watch of the night Jesus went to them, walking on the sea. And when the disciples saw Him walking on the sea, they were troubled, saying, "It is a ghost!" And they cried out for fear. But immediately Jesus spoke to them, saying, "Be of good cheer! It is I; do not be afraid."*
> MATTHEW 14:25-27

Remember, when we are in the middle of a great trial, when our flesh is weak, or Satan is waging a spiritual warfare against us, Jesus knows exactly what is happening. In His perfect timing, He will come to us right in the middle of our storms. Jesus brings peace in the midst of our storm to calm us, just like He did for His disciples.

When the disciples saw Jesus coming to them, they were reassured. Peter boldly asked the Lord: *"Lord, if it is You, command me to come to You on the water." So He said, "Come." And when Peter had come down out of the boat, he walked on the water to go to Jesus* (Matthew 14:28-29).

By faith, Peter stepped out of the boat and walked on the water. As long as his eyes were on the Lord and not on the storm, he was safe on the surface of the water. But when he took His eyes off Jesus and focused on the waves crashing around him, he got into trouble:

> *But when he saw that the wind was boisterous, he was afraid; and beginning to sink he cried out, saying, "Lord, save me!" And immediately Jesus stretched out His hand and caught him, and said to him, "O you of little faith, why did you doubt?" And when they got into the boat, the wind ceased.*
> MATTHEW 14:30-32

The storm did not subside until Jesus and Peter entered the boat. When Peter walked on the water, around him were huge, crashing waves, but he remained on the surface of the water. Peter was focused on Jesus, not the storm. His faith and trust was in Jesus, and he was able to walk on the water. He had no fear.

When Peter took his eyes off Jesus, and instead, placed his sight on the wind and waves, fear flooded into his life. Peter started to sink. In this single moment, he was not relying on the Lord. Fear took over. Peter would have sunk all the way down, if Jesus had not taken his hand.

We can learn so much from Peter's life and experiences. If we focus on the trials, tribulations, temptations and persecutions of this world, we too, will be paralyzed by fear.

Do not let your problems obscure your view of the Lord. You must not be so consumed and distraught by the spiritual battles you find yourself engaged in. When we fix our eyes on our problems and situations, often we cannot see Jesus—but He is there to fight for us.

No matter what storm is happening in our lives, Jesus will reach out to us and give us a helping hand. In Jesus Christ, we have the victory!

Chapter 8

JESUS IS VICTOR!

But thanks be to God, who gives us the victory through our Lord Jesus Christ. Therefore, my beloved brethren, be steadfast, immovable, always abounding in the work of the Lord, knowing that your labor is not in vain in the Lord.
1 CORINTHIANS 15:57-58

When a deadly enemy is defeated, the people rejoice. No matter how brutal the battlefield, victory brings joy. Although the mission is accomplished, it is bittersweet, as there are always casualties on both sides.

At the end of World War II, American newspapers announced these joyful headlines: "Victory!" "Germany Gives Up" "VE Day!" On May 8, 1945, President Harry Truman announced to the American people, that victory had happened in Europe. The Germans had surrendered to the allied forces. The President set aside May 13, 1945, which was Mother's

Day, as a day of prayer and thanksgiving. In his speech, he told the American people:

> "Our rejoicing is sobered and subdued by a supreme consciousness of the terrible price we have paid to rid the world of Hitler and his evil band. Let us not forget, my fellow Americans, the sorrow and the heartache which today abide in the homes of so many of our neighbors—neighbors whose most priceless possession has been rendered as a sacrifice to redeem our liberty . . . If I could give you a single watchword for the coming months, that word is work, work, and more work. We must work to finish the war—our victory is but half won . . . ."
>
> —PRESIDENT HARRY TRUMAN

America was still at war with Japan. Yet, despite the somber tone of the President's speech, spontaneous joy broke out, and 2,000,000 people swarmed the streets of New York City's Times Square in celebration of the European victory. It was a day of rejoicing. People danced in the streets amid the millions of flying pieces of paper that were thrown out of the high-rise windows. The sound of church bells rang out as the joyful news spread across the country. Celebrations continued throughout the following days.

Life Magazine described the day: " . . . it was as if joy had been rationed and saved up for the three years, eight months and seven days since Sunday, December 7, 1941"—when Pearl Harbor was attacked.

As the news of Japan's surrender to the allies was announced on August 14, 1945, known as VJ Day, the day Japan surrendered, America once again took to the streets in celebration. The people of America were jubilant—the war was finally ended! They waved American flags and showed the V for Victory sign with their hands. The noise of firecrackers filled the air and young boys and girls freely grabbed and kissed each other. This is when *Life Magazine's* famous photograph was captured of the sailor spontaneously kissing a nurse in Manhattan's Times Square. All these joyful and lasting memories are recorded in time.

The *Richmond Time-Dispatch* reminded its readers that, "The joy which is felt over the Japanese surrender should be tempered by a realization that this triumph was purchased at a frightful cost."

President Harry S. Truman commemorated Victory Day on September 2, 1945, as a holiday when a formal surrender ceremony was observed. Later, due to the good relations between America and Japan, the holiday was removed.

In comparison, the arduous War of Vietnam lasted from November 1, 1955, to April 30, 1975. It was one of the longest wars America has ever been involved in. The Marines in our unit dreamed of the day when they would be reunited with their wives and children. Fighting in the war was difficult, but the thought of loved ones at home kept our hopes alive. One day, this war and carnage would be over, and we could return home. These thoughts brought us so much joy. Home—a place where there would be happiness after so much suffering.

On January 23, 1973, Richard Nixon broadcasted an agreement that would bring about peace and honor in Vietnam and in South Asia. The agreement would cause an end to the war, and finally our American soldiers could come home. Most men returning to America envisioned a warm reception. They had fought for their country and for the freedom of the people at home and abroad.

An estimated 58,220 American soldiers died on the battlefields of Vietnam. These brave men and women paid the ultimate price—their lives. In Vietnam, 42 of my friends lost their lives. We had spent so much time going everywhere together. We ate, slept and fought as one. It hurt so much when they died; they gave their lives for our country.

Yet, unlike previous wars, when our troops returned home, it was not a joyous reunion. There were no celebrations or parades in the streets. In fact, many Military men and women returned to a very hostile environment. Tragically, these brave soldiers were not welcomed home because of the liberal media, which had portrayed the war in a very negative light. People were against the war, and they were against us. Military personnel returning from Vietnam were humiliated; people spat on them. While holding anti-war slogans, war protesters screamed obscenities and called us baby killers. Yet, we went to war to fight for freedom! So many people paid with their blood for this beautiful country.

Many soldiers returning from war suffered nightmares and PTSD—a mental disorder stemming from the trauma of being in war. These heroic men and women had a hard time adjusting back to civilian life. Many, especially those who were rejected by society, turned to alcohol and drugs. Sadly, these courageous vets are still found on our streets, jobless and homeless—how sad is that!

Marines wounded in battle returned to the United States only to find they had been abandoned by their wives. Soldiers often came back home without their limbs; their wives could not cope with a husband who had been severely wounded. Mistreated and dejected, Marines suffered considerable emotional pain. Many felt worthless, and without finding any meaning to life, they committed suicide. It is estimated that at least 20 Vietnam vets commit suicide each day.

RECOGNIZED AND HONORED

Even though most of society at the time did not show any recognition or honor to these heroic men and women who served their country and fought in Vietnam, Marines were recognized and honored for their acts of bravery on the battlefield. Our superior officers decorated them with medals in an official ceremony. Honor was given to whom it was due. Individual Marines were gratefully awarded, and as the officer looked straightforward into our eyes with great pride, he gave a firm handshake of thanks and recognition. Humbly, I, myself, being wounded twice in battle was awarded with commemorative medals and decorated with two Purple Hearts. I did what any other Marine would do for me in battle—we willingly laid down our lives for one another.

The Purple Heart is one of the most recognized and respected medals. It is awarded to members of the U.S. armed forces. It was first introduced as the Badge of Military Merit by General George Washington in 1782. The Purple Heart is also the nation's oldest military award. In military terms, the award had "broken service," as it was ignored for nearly 150 years until it was re-introduced on February 22, 1932, on the 200th anniversary of George Washington's birth. The medal's plain inscription, FOR MILITARY MERIT, barely conveys its significance.

—DEPARTMENT OF VETERANS AFFAIRS

The Vietnam Veteran Memorial Wall was dedicated in Washington DC, on November 13, 1982, to honor the courage and sacrifice of the military men and women who gave their lives in the war. Years later, my friends in combat and I visited the wall, looked for the names of those we lost, and wept together . . .

THE CROSS

Our heavenly Father gave to us His precious Only Son (John 3:16). Selflessly, Jesus willingly left the comfort of His eternal home to fight a spiritual battle on earth. He submissively did the work and will of His Father (John 4:34). Jesus' battlefield was brutal. His accepted mission was to go to the cross, where He would willingly become the only acceptable sacrifice for the forgiveness of our sins. His triumph on the cross redeemed our spiritual liberty, but at a high cost—His life. He won the battle. His priceless blood purchased for us:

> . . . knowing that you were not redeemed with corruptible things, like silver or gold, from your aimless conduct received by tradition from your fathers, but with the precious blood of Christ, as of a lamb without blemish and without spot. He indeed was foreordained before the foundation of the world, but was manifest in these last times for you
>
> I PETER 1:18-20

We read many of these Scriptures about Christ's sacrifice on the cross, but what did that violent battlefield for the souls of men look like? What really happened? What were the things that Jesus had to go through in order for us to be free—to receive salvation and eternal life?

Jesus' time of suffering began with betrayal. Judas, who had walked with the Lord for three and a half years as one of His twelve disciples, went to the chief priests and betrayed Him for thirty pieces of silver. In those days, it was the same amount of money for which you could purchase a slave. After Judas had been with Jesus for so long, and had seen His miracles—His wonders, His kindness, His love and His mercies—how could he have betrayed Him? Judas was never a true disciple of Jesus Christ! He had rejected Jesus and betrayed Him. Yet God was in control; His Word would be fulfilled.

Jesus knew His hour had come—the time of His suffering. He kept the Passover with His disciples, and as He sat down with the twelve, He told them that one of them was going to betray Him. They were all sorrowful, and, looking at each other, they wondered who the Lord was speaking about. Jesus identified His betrayer: "*He who dipped his hand with Me in the dish will betray Me*" (Matthew 26:23). Then Judas got up and quickly left. Meanwhile, Jesus instituted a new covenant:

And as they were eating, Jesus took bread, blessed and broke it, and gave it to the disciples and said, "Take, eat; this is My body." Then He took the cup, and gave thanks, and gave it to them,

saying, "Drink from it, all of you. For this is My blood of the new covenant, which is shed for many for the remission of sins.
MATTHEW 26:26-28

Jesus and the disciples began to sing a Psalm and then left the house (Matthew 26:30). Psalms 113-118 are called the Hallel—meaning praise, a series of Psalms that were traditionally sung at the Passover meal. Then Jesus revealed to them:

"All of you will be made to stumble because of Me this night, for it is written: 'I will strike the Shepherd, And the sheep of the flock will be scattered.' But after I have been raised, I will go before you to Galilee."
MATTHEW 26:31, 32

Peter, hearing the Lord's words, pledged he would never deny the Lord, and all the other disciples agreed. But Jesus looked at Peter and foretold him of his denial (Matthew 26:33-35). Entering into the Garden of Gethsemane, Jesus prayed for God's will to be done: *And being in agony, He prayed more earnestly. Then His sweat became like great drops of blood falling down to the ground* (Luke 22:44).

The disciples, however, slept and failed to pray (Matthew 26:40, 43, 46). Now, the hateful crowd, not the loving crowd, approached. Judas the traitor—one of His own—led over 600 men with torches, clubs and swords. Judas was leading the pack of all those who hated Jesus (Matthew 26:47).

Judas, in the company of these wicked men, came with great confidence to give Jesus a kiss of betrayal. It was not just a peck but he continuously kissed Jesus until the Lord interrupted Him, as if to say, "Stop Judas. Do what you have come to do." How sad. (Matthew 26:49, 50; Luke 22:47, 48).

Then, *samurai* Peter drew his sword and cut off Malchus' ear (John 18:10). I believe he was going for the head, but he only got this servant's right ear. In John 18:11, Jesus told Peter: *Put your sword into the sheath. Shall I not drink the cup which My Father has given Me?"* Matthew 26:53 tells us that Jesus could have called on more than twelve legions of angels! Can you imagine twelve legions of angels? A legion is a term for 6,000 Roman soldiers, so the Lord could have called up more than 72,000 angels! When you consider that one angel killed 185,000 men from an Assyrian army (Isaiah 37:36, 37), the amount of angels Jesus could have summoned would have killed everybody on earth!

Jesus Faces His Enemies

Jesus was arrested and led away to Caiaphas. In fear, all the disciples abandoned Him. Jesus would face three people alone who were His enemies: Jesus was first led to Annas a high priest and then to his son-in-law Caiaphas, who replaced him as high priest, (John 18:13, 14), and finally to Pilate, a Roman governor. At Caiaphas' house, the Jewish leaders held a midnight trial. This trial was not legal under Jewish law; Jesus would be illegally confronted.

The Jewish leaders' plot was to look for false witnesses who would be willing to lie against Jesus. The chief priest interrogated the Lord, *"Do You answer nothing? What is it these men testify against You?"* Jesus kept silent. Caiaphas gave another direct question to Jesus: *"I put You under oath by the living God: Tell us if You are the Christ, the Son of God!"* (Matthew 26:57, 62, 63).

Excuse me? The Living God is right in front of you! In return, Jesus gave the high priest a direct answer: *"It is as you said. Nevertheless, I say to you, hereafter you will see the Son of Man sitting at the right hand of the power, and coming on the clouds of heaven"* (Matthew 26:64). Jesus had opened His mouth and given a full testimony of His deity.

The Jewish leader reacted with extreme emotion and great expression. The high priest tore his clothing while accusing Jesus of blasphemy. In his opinion, Jesus was deserving of death, but Jesus was not guilty. In contempt, these leaders who had gathered against Him spat in His face. In Israel, it was an extreme insult to spit in someone's face. Then they placed a sack over His head and began to abuse, beat and mock Him. Finally, in the morning, they delivered Him to the Roman governor, Pontius Pilate (Matthew 26:65-67; 27:2).

Pilate was completely aware of the truth behind the religious leaders' actions. They were envious of Jesus; however, Pilate was willing to make a compromise with them. He was afraid his position as governor would be taken away from him by Caesar. To appease the crowds, Pilate made an offer; he could release Barabbas, a murderer and an assassin, or the Christ—the Anointed One of God (Matthew 27:15-18).

Let me ask you this, "At this time, where were all the people who Jesus healed, those whom He ministered to, and the multitudes He had fed?" Everybody had turned against Him—how sad is that!

Pilate chose to please the Jews and buckled under pressure to their demands to crucify Jesus. He would not step up to the plate and release Him. Instead, he washed his hands of this Just Person. He released Barabbas and gave the order for Jesus to be scourged and crucified (Matthew 27:19-26).

Jesus was taken to a place where there was a pole in the ground that had rings near the top. His hands and arms were put through and tied up. His legs were spread and His back exposed. The leather whip used to scourge Jesus had animal teeth, iron, metal and even glass attached to the end. As the soldiers would strike the prisoner, the whip would wrap around the back to the front and rip off His skin—shredding His flesh.

A prisoner was given 40 lashes and with every strike, they would have to confess their sins—Jesus had no sin. Jesus had already made His confession—He was the King of Kings. They had rejected Him. So, the Lord was given 39 lashes, the number of mercy. By the time Jesus had received 39 lashes, you could properly see the white bone of His back. Isaiah 53:2 describes Jesus' mutilation: . . . *He has no form or comeliness; and when we see Him, there is no beauty that we should desire Him.*

Then a detachment of soldiers, about 600 men (John 18:3), came and surrounded one innocent Man! They stripped Jesus of His clothing and humiliated Him. The soldiers placed a scarlet robe on Jesus to mock Him as the King of the Jews. They had no fear or respect for Him. Then they twisted a crown of thorns and rammed it into his skull. The Palestinian plants had thorns that were three inches long and very sharp.

Imagine, Jesus blood must have poured down His face, into His eyes and cheeks, as blood mingled with His beard. As a scepter, they gave Him a reed and laughed and mocked Him as the King of the Jews. The soldiers continued to abuse Jesus as they spat on Him and plucked out His beard. They took the thin reed and began to slap Him hard on the head (Isaiah 50:6; Matthew 27:27-30).

The Roman soldiers walked Jesus through the streets of Jerusalem thronged with people. He experienced the shame as He carried His cross among the screaming crowds. Simon, a man of Cyrene, was compelled by the soldiers to carry His cross (Matthew 27:31, 32).

Jesus was then taken outside of the city to Golgotha—also known as the Place of a Skull—to be crucified with two thieves (Matthew 27:33, 38). Jesus would have been laid down on the cross as they took these huge nails—spikes—and put them through His hands and feet. The cross was placed upright and dropped into a three-foot hole in the ground, and as they dropped it, His armpits would have ripped. Can you imagine the ripping of His arms—the agonizing pain?

Pilate wrote a title, in three different languages, put it on sign and fixed it on the cross: JESUS OF NAZARETH, THE KING OF THE JEWS. *Then many of the Jews read this title, for the place where Jesus was crucified was near the city; and it was written in Hebrew, Greek, and Latin* (John 19:19, 20).

As Jesus hung there bleeding, those who came by wagged their heads out of utter disgust and hatred. They and the Jewish leaders, even the robbers, ridiculed Him and continued their mocking, mocking, mocking . . . (Matthew 27:39-44).

As Jesus took the sins of the world upon Himself, the Father turned His back on His Son. In Mathew 27:46 Jesus cried out: *"My God, My God, why have You forsaken Me?"*

Jesus endured the cross and took the penalty for our sins because of His unconditional love for us. Jesus took full responsibility for our sins. If we respond to His love, and accept His forgiveness, He will give you His everlasting life.

Christ's Day of Victory

Once Christ had cried out, *"It is finished!"* and died (John 19:30), Jesus had won the war against Satan. He was a defeated enemy. The victory is won and the war is over; the price has been paid for our sins—it is a done deal! Jesus had died physically, but He triumphed over death, as He would resurrect on the third day.

Satan thought he had won the battle when Jesus died on the cross. But Jesus, after His death descended into hell, preached the Gospel to those held captive there until His resurrection (Luke 16:19-31), . . . *He* [Christ] *ascended on high, He led captivity captive, and gave gifts to men"* (Ephesians 4:7-10). Satan then knew he had been defeated.

What Christ's victory accomplished on the cross is written in Hebrews 2:14, 15:

Inasmuch then as the children have partaken of flesh and blood, He [Jesus] *Himself likewise shared in the same, that through death He might destroy him who had the power of death, that is, the devil, and release those who through fear of death were all their lifetime subject to bondage.*

Christ's victorious resurrection means we no longer need to be afraid to die! Death has been conquered, amazing, amazing. The Apostle Paul speaking of the resurrection of the dead expounds for us further:

So when this corruptible has put on incorruption, and this mortal has put on immortality, then shall be brought to pass the saying that is written: "Death is swallowed up in victory." "O Death, where is your sting? O Hades, where is your victory?" The sting of death is sin, and the strength of sin is the law. But thanks be to God, who gives us the victory through our Lord Jesus Christ.

I CORINTHIANS 15:54-57

Now, anybody can come to Jesus to receive everlasting life! Did you know that when one sinner repents of their sins and accepts Christ, there is a joyous celebration in heaven? In Luke 15:10, Jesus said: *"Likewise, I say to you, there is joy in the presence of the angels of God over one sinner who repents."* Yet, so many people prepare for everything else in life except death! Militarily wise, we need to look at life as short-timers—like those in Vietnam who only had less than two months to serve before returning home. Seriously, people die at any age, young or old it does not matter; so we need to be ready—you want to make sure your bags are packed.

JOY, DESPITE THE CROSS

When Jesus faced the cross, know this; He still had joy. Jesus kept His joy because He knew, after His death, He would be reunited with the Father (John 17:4, 5). In our lives, no matter what we face, we need to constantly look to Jesus as our example. We need to retain our joy and endure our earthly trials, because we are assured of our heavenly destination:

> . . . *looking unto Jesus, the author and finisher of our faith, who for the joy that was set before Him endured the cross, despising the shame, and has sat down at the right hand of the throne of God.*
>
> HEBREWS 12:2

Despite our trials, remember God is still on the throne!

JESUS OVERCAME THE WORLD

When Jesus came to this earth, He experienced great trials, great tribulations, great temptations and great persecution. Satan tried to make Him turn from the Father. Many people came against Jesus; He knew He would be hated by the world He came to save. Not only did the world hate Him, but the people of the world would hate His followers. That is why He left His disciples with this warning:

> *"If the world hates you, you know that it hated Me before it hated you. If you were of the world, the world would love its*

own. Yet because you are not of the world, but I chose you out of the world, therefore the world hates you."

JOHN 15:18, 19

Jesus did not want His disciples or us to be surprised when persecution came. He wanted us to know that we would face trials; similar to the trials He endured in His time on this earth:

"Remember the word that I said to you, 'A servant is not greater than his master.' If they persecuted Me, they will also persecute you. If they kept My word, they will keep yours also. But all these things they will do to you for My name's sake, because they do not know Him who sent Me."

JOHN 15:20, 21

Before Christ went to the cross, He told His disciples the reality of becoming one of His followers. They were told to expect trials, tribulations, temptations, persecution and suffering; but they should not focus on those things, because Jesus had promised them, *" . . . in Me you may have peace. In the world you will have tribulation; but be of good cheer, I have overcome the world"* (John 16:33).

Despite the battles we are engaged in, these are reassuring words from the Lord. He identified with everything we will ever experience in life, and He overcame it. We may not have peace in this world, but we can have peace in Him—I love the heart of Jesus.

In the Christian walk, Jesus Christ never promised His followers an easy life. Following Jesus will bring a challenge to every child of God, because they will enter into great spiritual warfare. Satan was defeated by Christ at the cross, but he still wages a spiritual warfare against you and me. It is important to remember, when the battles come, we have victory in Jesus—Jesus is victor! As He overcame the world, we also can overcome the world, through Him. First John 5:4 tells us: *For whatever is born of God overcomes the world. And this is the victory that has overcome the world—our faith.*

REJOICE IN THE BATTLE

It is very important to understand that joy does not come from our outward circumstances. It comes from the inward relationship we have with the Lord. In actuality, it is one of the fruit of the Spirit*: But the fruit of the Spirit is love, joy, peace, longsuffering, kindness, goodness, faithfulness, gentleness, self-control . . .* (Galatians 5:22, 23).

We know as believers in Christ, we are engaged in spiritual warfare, but we do not have to be discouraged. We have to pray and know God's Word. In the middle of every battle, these things will strengthen us and encourage us. In the midst of the battle, it is also good to remember we are not alone. A great encouragement to believers as they continue to battle in a spiritual war is James 1:2, 3: *My brethren, count it all joy when you fall into various trials, knowing that the testing of your faith produces patience.*

God does not want us to be sad when we face hard trials in life. Knowing that our God will help us to overcome our circumstances, we should rejoice!

> "Joy is delight at God's grace which enables us
> to endure our trials."
> GEORGE SEEVERS

The Apostle Paul experienced and understood the tremendous spiritual battle every Christian will engage in during their lifetime. He wrote these great words as a reminder and encouragement to the Church:

Therefore, having been justified by faith, we have peace with God through our Lord Jesus Christ, through whom also we have access by faith into this grace in which we stand, and rejoice in hope of the glory of God. And not only that, but we also glory in tribulations, knowing that tribulation produces perseverance; and perseverance, character; and character, hope. Now hope does not disappoint, because the love of God has been poured out in our hearts by the Holy Spirit who was given to us.

ROMANS 5:1-5

Our victory in Jesus is the most important thing we have in this world. Without the Scriptures' assurance, we would be a people without hope. We would go through this life hopeless, without joy.

In the Book of Philippians, Paul, a prisoner of Jesus Christ, never once murmured or complained under the circumstances and situations that God allowed him to be in—even prison. In the conclusion of this Book, he writes to us from a dungeon in Rome, to encourage us to rejoice in the Lord, which is hard to do especially if you are going through difficult circumstances. One of the things I have found about Paul is that, even though he was in chains, he never had his eyes on his circumstances, and that is why he could write: *Rejoice in the Lord always. Again I will say, rejoice!* (Philippians 4:4)

SUFFERING FOR CHRIST

The Book of Acts records the situation when Peter and other apostles had just been beaten by the Jewish council. Why did they suffer? It was because they were Christians, and they were preaching and teaching in the name of Jesus. They had already been told . . . *not to speak at all nor teach in the name of Jesus* (Acts 4:18).

Listening to God rather than men, Peter and John once again preached Christ. In Act 5:28, the high priest angrily addressed them, *saying, "Did we not strictly command you not to teach in this name? And look, you have filled Jerusalem with your doctrine, and intend to bring this Man's blood on us!"*

After the Jewish leaders asked wise counsel from Gamaliel, a Pharisee who taught Saul, later to become Paul, they called for the apostles and beat them. Then they commanded that they should not speak in the name of Jesus, and let them go (Acts 5:40).

The Apostles rejoiced in their sufferings. They did not go on their way murmuring or complaining. We find the reason in Acts 5:41: *So they departed from the presence of the council, rejoicing that they were counted worthy to suffer shame for His name.* The Apostles counted it as a blessing and a privilege to suffer for Christ.

In Acts 9 Saul, a persecutor of the Church, had a dramatic conversion to Christ and the Lord changed his name to Paul. He would be used of the Lord to preach the Gospel to the Gentiles. Ananias was told to pray for Paul who would suffer for Christ: *"Go, for he is a chosen vessel of Mine to bear My name before Gentiles, kings, and the children of Israel. For I will show him how many things he must suffer for My name's sake"* (Acts 9:15-16).

Paul the Apostle was a man who really understood what it meant to suffer for Christ. He wrote 14 Epistles and shared about the many difficulties he had experienced in his Christian life to encourage us.

Paul explained to the Christians in Rome:

The Spirit Himself bears witness with our spirit that we are children of God, and if children, then heirs—heirs of God and joint heirs with Christ, if indeed we suffer with Him, that we may also be glorified together. For I consider that the sufferings of this present time are not worthy to be compared with the glory which shall be revealed in us.

ROMANS 8:16-18

Honestly, whatever we are going through today does not compare to heaven's glory. As a child of God, you will suffer for His sake. You will not only suffer, but you will find joy in the suffering, because in the end you will be glorified with the Lord. Seriously, if Jesus suffered for you, why should you not suffer for Him?

When you suffer for Jesus Christ, it is never in vain; nothing we do for the Lord is in vain:

But thanks be to God, who gives us the victory through our Lord Jesus Christ. Therefore, my beloved brethren, be steadfast, immovable, always abounding in the work of the Lord, knowing that your labor is not in vain in the Lord.

1 CORINTHIANS 15:57, 58

Paul told the believers in the Philippian church: *For to you it has been granted on behalf of Christ, not only to believe in Him, but also to suffer for His sake* (Philippians 1:29).

211

It is after Christ's example that we suffer . . . *that I may know Him and the power of His resurrection, and the fellowship of His sufferings, being conformed to His death* . . . (Philippians 3:10).

Paul encouraged the believers in Thessalonica for their testimony of suffering:

> *And you became followers of us and of the Lord, having received the word in much affliction, with joy of the Holy Spirit, so that you became examples to all in Macedonia and Achaia who believe.*
> 1 THESSALONIANS 1:6, 7

In everything we are going through, Christ is our example. God will give you peace and strength in everything you are facing. When things happen to me, they happen according to God's plan. Peter said: . . . *but rejoice to the extent that you partake of Christ's sufferings, that when His glory is revealed, you may also be glad with exceeding joy* (1 Peter 4:13).

Peter also gives to us the reason for a hopeful attitude:

> *But may the God of all grace, who called us to His eternal glory by Christ Jesus, after you have suffered a while, perfect, establish, strengthen, and settle you.*
> 1 PETER 5:10

He reminds us that God's grace is real. We are called to know that we are going into glory! We do not like suffering but everybody suffers. We may not understand suffering, but God uses suffering to equip us and build a solid foundation of faith in our lives. We learn that God is on the throne and that everything we go through will bring glory and honor to Christ:

HONORED BY CHRIST

The Lord had sent His disciples to witness to other people. He had equipped them and sent them out, two by two, into the world. Before they went, He began to warn them about persecution.

We need to understand that believers are going to be tested in regards to their faith. Faithful disciples must be tried. I can remember back in the Jesus people movement everyone shared their faith; it is something that seems to be coming to an end. Christians are not sharing their faith with people. I believe God is going to initiate something in the future, whereby the faith of people will be challenged.

America is changing very rapidly; we are living in strange days. More and more of our laws are changing; these laws have come against the Church and the Word of God. In the future, your children and your children's children will have to face all these issues. There is a war going on against pastors and against the Church. It might be that there is a time coming where the churches close down and pastors go to jail!

Know one thing: God controls such persecution and any dangerous events that happen. Christ cares for every minute detail in our lives; that is why He tells us not to fear. As persecution or problems develop in our lives, the Lord will be there for us, because He is God Almighty. In every pain, injury or affliction, He will help us. If we have committed any sin, we are forgiven. He does not bring us to shame—He brings us to the cross of Jesus Christ. He shows us that we truly have been forgiven—cleansed and washed. He makes us ready to go to heaven.

Jesus spoke about confessing Him in the most difficult moments imaginable, not denying Him when you are being persecuted. Notice what Christ says:

> *Therefore whoever confesses me before men, him I will also confess before my Father who is in heaven. But whoever denies me before men, him I will also deny before my Father who is in heaven.*
>
> MATTHEW 10:32, 33

Jesus Christ will honor those who have confessed their belief in Him before men, and He will honor them before His Father and all the angels in heaven. We cannot be ashamed of Christ:

> *"For whoever is ashamed of Me and My words in this adulterous and sinful generation, of him the Son of Man also*

will be ashamed when He comes in the glory of His Father with the holy angels."

MARK 8:38

Interesting! So if you are ashamed now to be a Christian and to share with others about eternity, how can you expect God to honor your life? Will you choose to follow Christ, deny yourself, pick up your cross, and follow Him? You need to lose your life for Jesus' sake and the Gospel. When you pick up your cross, the instrument of death, and follow Jesus, you are making an eternal investment, not wasting your life on temporal things.

Seriously, you need to come to some crucial conclusions in your life. Do you love Christ? How much to do value your soul? Make a decision to follow Jesus and let go of everything else.

REWARDED BY CHRIST

The Apostle Paul shared that one day, each one of us are going to have to stand in the presence of God, to receive a reward for the works that He had committed to us to complete. What did God call us to do? Using our gifts and talents, what have we built eternally? Our life's work will be reviewed; it will either endure or be lost:

For we are God's fellow workers; you are God's field, you are God's building. According to the grace of God which was given to me, as a wise master builder I have laid the foundation, and another builds on it. But let each one take heed how he builds on it. For no other foundation can anyone lay than that which is laid, which is Jesus Christ. Now if anyone builds on this foundation with gold, silver, precious stones, wood, hay, straw, each one's work will become clear; for the Day [the judgment Day of Christ] will declare it, because it will be revealed by fire; and the fire will test each one's work, of what sort it is. If anyone's work which he has built on it endures, he will receive a reward. If anyone's work is burned, he will suffer loss; but he himself will be saved, yet so as through fire.

1 CORINTHIANS 3:9-14

Paul is speaking about the Bema Seat of Christ where Jesus Christ will give judgment to every believer for whatever works they were entrusted with, while on earth. Fire will test the quality of our works. What materials did we use to build?

As the Scriptures declare, the materials that will be tested are gold, silver, precious stones, wood, hay, and straw (1 Corinthians 3:9-14). As our works are cast into the fire, they will be examined and evaluated to see what value they have. For example: Why did you go to church, pray, and read your Bible? Did you apply what was read? How did you manage your finances? Why did you give to God? Did you do all these things with a pure heart? Jesus Christ will judge our hearts and motives.

If you had wrong motives or a bad attitude, then nothing will remain from the fire. If nothing comes out of the fire then, you will still be saved as by the fire, but you will not reign with Christ for a thousand years when He comes back to the earth. But you will make it into the kingdom of God because of Christ's death on the cross for the forgiveness of sin. Revelation 20:6 speaks of Christ's victorious reign: *Blessed and holy is* he who has part in the first resurrection. Over such the second death has no power, but they shall be priests of God and of Christ, and shall reign with Him a thousand years (Revelation 20:6).

In Romans 14:10-12, Paul gave to us another reference to the Bema Seat of Christ:

But why do you judge your brother? Or why do you show contempt for your brother? For we shall all stand before the judgment seat of Christ. For it is written: "As I live, says the Lord, every knee shall bow to Me, and every tongue shall confess to God." So then each of us shall give account of himself to God.

Then again, when Paul spoke about death, he informed us: *For we must all appear before the judgment seat of Christ, that each one may receive the things done* in the body, according to what he has done, whether good or *bad* (2 Corinthians 5:10). Every one of us will die one day that is a real fact; no one will escape death in this life. Some people die when they are young, some die older and others live to be a

100 years old. But every person, no matter what age, will die one day. Once we die, then the judgment comes.

Billy Graham stated: "The Bible says there is no possible way of escape. Sooner or later we must leave our dream world and face up to the fact of God and sin and judgment."

How beautiful to be judged from the righteousness of Jesus Christ. This is why David said: Blessed is he whose transgression is forgiven, whose sin is covered (Psalm 32:1). Paul in Ephesians 1:7 tells us: *In Him* [Christ] *we have redemption through His blood, the forgiveness of sins, according to the riches of His grace.*

Christians shall not have to stand at the Great White Throne Judgment, the last judgment, as the non-believer. They did not place their faith in Jesus Christ. According to John the Beloved, in the Book of Revelation, they will have a different judgment.

Then I saw a great white throne and Him who sat on it, from whose face the earth and the heaven fled away. And there was found no place for them. And I saw the dead, small and great, standing before God, and books were opened. And another book was opened, which is the Book of Life. And the dead were judged according to their works, by the things which were written in the books. The sea gave up the dead who were in it, and Death and Hades delivered up the dead who were in them. And they were judged, each one according to his works. *Then Death and Hades were cast into the lake of*

*fire. This is the second death. And anyone not found written
in the Book of Life was cast into the lake of fire.*

REVELATION 20:11-15

Remember, those who have accepted Christ as Lord and
Savior, have their original sin forgiven at the Cross. My sins
and your sins were nailed to the Cross of Christ. We shall
never stand in the presence of God to be judged for our
sins, it will only be for the works that God intended for us to
complete, as Children of the Light.

I take my call as a pastor, in giving to you the Word of
God, seriously. I know in the time to come you will have to
stand alone, in the presence of God, to give an account of
your life. We temporarily live in the world. The life to come is
eternal—we shall never die ever again and I want you to be
ready. Hebrews 9:27 makes this clear: *And as it is appointed
for men to die once, but after this the judgment.*

THE VICTOR'S CROWN

Jesus wore a twisted crown of thorns on His head as He
was crucified, but in Hebrews 2:9, our Conquering Christ was
crowned in glory and honor:

*But we see Jesus, who was made a little lower than the angels,
for the suffering of death crowned with glory and honor, that
He, by the grace of God, might taste death for everyone.*

219

The Bible mentions five crowns that can be given to believers at the Bema Seat of Christ in eternity. First there is the Imperishable Crown. These believers crucified their life to the cross of Jesus Christ. They brought their flesh under submission and did not live a life of carnality or give in to sin. They had a disciplined life and stood by God's Word: *And everyone who competes for the prize is temperate in all things. Now they do it to obtain a perishable crown, but we for an imperishable crown* (1 Corinthians 9:25).

Athletes who go to the Olympics have to train, and make sacrifices. They discipline their lives for years before they compete for the gold or silver medal—that is a great accomplishment. Paul says that is nothing, we are seeking for the crown that is incorruptible.

Second, the Crown of Rejoicing is a crown for soul winning—think about that! First Thessalonians 2:19 says: *For what is* our hope, or joy, or crown of rejoicing? *Is it* not even you in the presence of our Lord Jesus Christ at His coming?

Third, the Crown of Righteousness is given to those who love the coming of the Lord. Christians who are looking and living for the coming of the Lord: *Finally, there is laid up for me the crown of righteousness, which the Lord, the righteous Judge, will give to me on that Day, and not to me only but also to all who have loved His appearing* (2 Timothy 4:7, 8).

Fourth, the Crown of Life, this crown will be given to those who will pass the tests of life—trials and temptations: *"Blessed is the man who endures temptation; for when he has been approved, he will receive the crown of life which the Lord has promised to those who love Him* (James 1:12).

Fifth, and lastly, the Crown of Glory, according to 1 Peter 5:4, this is given to faithful pastors. Those who have fed and have shepherded the flock of God: *and when the Chief Shepherd appears, you will receive the crown of glory that does not fade away.*

Then the Bible describes a heavenly scene where twenty-four elders cast their crowns at the feet of Jesus:

The twenty-four elders fall down before Him who sits on the throne and worship Him who lives forever and ever, and cast their crowns before the throne, saying: "You are worthy, O Lord, to receive glory and honor and power; for You created all things, and by Your will they exist and were created."
REVELATION 4:10, 11

I love this, because Jesus is the one who deserves all honor, not us.

Our lifetime is so short; so we must be careful how we live our lives and invest into the kingdom of God. A crown is not given to you until you have been to the cross. Christians must work—work—work and make the best of the time we have been given to serve the Lord and share the Gospel message. Understand that it is only what we do for Christ that will last. Jesus said: *"Behold, I am coming quickly, and My* reward *is* with Me, to render to every man *according to what he has done"* (Revelation 22:12).

Always—always remember to fight the battle, and be a good soldier of Jesus Christ, because it is God who gives to us the victory through our Lord Jesus Christ. We are able to live a life of victory, die in victory and live forever in victory!

A MARINE'S TRIBUTE

Raul Ries was honored at a Dodgers' game on August 16, 2016. It was announced over the PA system:

"We would like to pay special tribute to the men and women of our nation's armed forces by honoring a military hero of the game. I am very proud to honor Pastor Raul Ries, Lance Corporal, who served in the U.S. Marine Corps from 1966 to1968. During the Vietnam War, Pastor Ries served in Alpha Company, 1st Battalion, 7th Marines, a highly trained group called the Bounty Hunters. His awards include the Vietnamese Service Campaign medals and two Purple Hearts. Today, Pastor Ries is the Senior Pastor of Calvary Chapel Golden Springs, with a congregation of more than 14,000, and his daily, syndicated, radio program called Somebody Loves You is heard on 350 radio stations, internationally. Pastor Ries, the Dodgers thank you for your service, sacrifice and dedication to our country, and we hope you have a great time at the ballpark tonight!"

God honors those who honor Him...

I will be with him in trouble;
I will deliver him and honor him.
With long life I will satisfy him,
and show him My salvation.

PSALM 91:16

Somebody Loves You Publishing Books

Raul Ries

From Fury to Freedom (revised)
From Fury to Freedom (audio book)
Man: Natural, Carnal, Spiritual
Impurity: The Naked Truth
Sin: The Root of All Evil
Obedience: Waking Up to God (devotional)
Doctrines: A Simplified Road Map of Biblical Truth
Doctrines: A Simplified Road Map of Biblical Truth (audio book)
Servant: The Person God Uses
Victory: Overcoming the Enemy
Seven Steps to a Successful Marriage
Seven Steps to a Successful Marriage (audio book)
Raising a Godly Family in an Ungodly World
Somebody Loves You Growth Book (booklet)
30 Questions that Deserve Answers (booklet)
Practical Living from God's Word Devotional
Understanding God's Compassion (booklet)
Living Above Your Circumstances:
    A Study in the Book of Daniel
Hear What the Spirit Is Saying

Chuck Smith

The Philosophy of Ministry: Calvary Chapel (Spanish also)

Sharon Ries

The Well-Trodden Path
My Husband, My Maker
The Night Cometh: Edmund and Naomi Farrel
Written Bible Studies (Spanish also)

Claire Wren

Crimson

DVDs

Raul Ries

Fury to Freedom
Taking the Hill: 2-DVD Package
A Quiet Hope
A Venture in Faith: The History and Philosophy of the
    Calvary Chapel Movement
      (all are available in Spanish)

Books & Pamphlets in Spanish

Doctrinas (pronto para estrenar)
El Pecado de la Ira
El Pecado de la Envidia
El Pecado de la Impureza
El Pecado de la Soberbia

Short Films

Shane Ries

The Parisian Incident
Cycle
W 3sixty5
Abraham's Desert

Base 9

www.base9.com@aol.com

Somebody Loves You Radio is the teaching ministry of Pastor Raul Ries. After committing his life to Christ in 1972, Raul has been driven to share the message of God's love to a lost and dying world.

Somebody Loves You Radio is a 30-minute daily show which is heard worldwide on over 350 stations and can also be found on the Somebody Loves You website, mobile app, and downloadable podcasts. The vision of Somebody Loves You is simple but powerful, to reach the world for Christ.

SOMEBODY LOVES YOU®

RADIO
WWW.SOMEBODYLOVESYOU.COM